PRAISE FOR

WHERE THERE IS HOPE, COURAGE, AND GRACE: THE JOURNEY TO ME

"A powerful reflection of resilience, grace, and personal growth. More than stories, it's a companion and catalyst for transformation."
~ Christina Arnold, LMSW

"Each chapter felt like a mirror—tears, deep sighs, and so much release. This book knew what I needed before I did."
~ Hope Davis

"Like therapy in written form—grounded, wise, and spiritually rich. Every chapter healed, and every Blooming Forward transformed me."
~ Rene Kelley

"A heart-to-heart with someone who's walked through fire and still chose to bloom. For anyone in transition, this book is wisdom, strength, and a path back to your voice."
~Yasmine Hamilton

"I saw myself in these pages—in the girl who needed protection and the woman who chose healing. This book gave voice to things I had tucked away and reminded me that my story still matters."
~Terria Herron, MS, ALC

WHERE THERE IS HOPE COURAGE AND GRACE

The Journey to Me

VICTORIA SEWELL

FOREWORD BY LASHUNDA WILSON MS, LPC, NCC

MAHOGANYBLUE
PUBLISHING

Published by Mahogany Blue Publishing LLC, P.O. Box 1213, Montgomery, Alabama 36102, USA

This book is intended for inspirational and personal growth purposes only. The author and publisher are not offering medical, psychological, or mental health advice. This book is not a substitute for professional diagnosis, treatment, or therapy. If you are experiencing mental health issues or medical conditions, please consult a qualified healthcare professional.

Scripture quotations are taken from the Holy Bible, New International Version®, NIV®. Copyright © 1973, 1978, 1984, 2011 by Biblica, Inc. ® Used by permission of Zondervan. All rights reserved worldwide.

Cover Designed by Beccas Dader

Cover Art Illustrated by Anna Ismagilova/ Adobe Stock

ISBN (Paperback): 979-8-9896792-0-1

ISBN (eBook): 979-8-9896792-4-9

First Edition, August 2025

Printed in the United States of America

*"You asked me if I ever stood up for anything.
Yeah, I stood up for my life."*
— Tina Turner, *Vanity Fair*, 1993

CONTENTS

FOREWORD

In every chapter of my career, from long nights in group homes with teenagers in foster care to counseling rooms where, after years of holding back, women finally let the tears come, I have witnessed how trauma shapes a life. I have seen how early abandonment echoes into adulthood, how unspoken grief hides behind high achievement, and how survival can become so automatic that true healing feels like a foreign language. Over time, I have learned that the bravest thing a person can do is not to endure alone but to allow themselves to be seen in their truth. That is why *Where There Is Hope, Courage, and Grace: The Journey to Me* matters. It transcends the boundaries of a book; it is a hand extended to anyone ready to step out of survival and into healing.

Before my work in private practice, I spent years serving youth in foster care, both in direct care and in administrative roles, walking alongside children and teens whose trust in the world had been fractured too soon. I saw firsthand how instability and unhealed wounds can follow a person into every corner of life, and how the right support at the right time can alter the entire course of someone's story. Those early experiences shaped the way I approach therapy today: with equal measures of clinical skill and deep respect for the courage it takes to begin again.

In my years as a licensed professional counselor, I have sat with women in transition from the heartbreak of divorce to the lasting pain of abuse, trauma, and generational wounds. I have been an empathetic witness to stories of survival, silence, and misplaced accountability. Many of these women, despite their strength, have felt trapped in cycles they could not name. They had mastered carrying the weight but had never been shown how to lay it down.

Research tells us that nearly one in three women will experience some form of trauma in their lifetime, whether through abuse, neglect, or abandonment. Far too many will navigate their pain in silence. In my counseling practice, I have seen how trauma often hides beneath high achievement, over-functioning, and relentless self-sacrifice. While the outside world praises these coping strategies, they can keep women locked in survival long after the events themselves have passed.

Time and again, I have met women who have done everything society asked of them; they have loved, sacrificed, and endured, and yet live with an ache they cannot quite name. They carry invisible wounds, stitched together by resilience but weighed down by secrets too heavy to keep forever. The cost of that silence is often a slow erosion of identity, joy, and a sense of belonging.

Through years of listening and holding space, I have learned that healing rarely begins with theory. It begins with testimony. It starts when a woman hears someone else speak a truth that mirrors her own. When she dares to reject what no longer serves her to reclaim her autonomy piece by piece and trust her voice again. That is what *Where There Is Hope, Courage, and Grace: The Journey to Me* offers.

Victoria Sewell does not write from detachment or abstraction. She writes from the marrow of lived experience. Her words are not written to be read alone, but to be felt. They pulse with honesty and grace, the kind that only emerges after surviving what could have broken her and choosing, instead, to heal.

As someone who knows Victoria personally and professionally, I can say without hesitation: this book is not just empowering, it's essential. A rare blend of memoir and guide, and a companion for anyone standing at the edge of change.

In my work, I often meet women who have learned to survive but have never been shown how to heal. They wear strength like armor, but beneath it, tenderness waits for the freedom to speak. Their vulnerability has been tucked away for years, sometimes decades. These women need tools along with a safe, nonjudgmental space to lay their truths down and rebuild from the inside out.

This book is that space.

Victoria leads us through her own becoming with compassion and courage, not as someone who has "arrived," but as someone willing to go first. She shows us what it means to find hope when the path is unclear, practice courage when your voice falters, and extend grace to the parts of yourself silenced by shame. And to return to the self you were always meant to be, not the version defined by others, but a woman grounded in her own worth.

She speaks to the woman who has survived more than she thought she could. To the woman who feels like a stranger to herself and the woman daring to believe that what lies ahead can be better than what she has left behind.

What makes this book extraordinary is that it's a testimony and a resource. It offers space for reflection, connection, and the slow but steady work of rebuilding. Victoria tells her story while inviting you into your own.

Through scripture, reflection prompts, and gentle encouragement, she creates a safe place for readers to pause, process, and begin again at their own pace, in their own way. Her words honor your timing, your process, and your humanity.

If you are in a season of rebuilding, navigating loss, heartbreak, or weary from holding yourself together, these pages will meet you where you are. They will walk with you, one chapter at a time, as you rediscover hope, courage, and grace in your own life.

Victoria, thank you for offering your voice so that other women might reclaim theirs. Thank you for reminding us that hope, courage, and grace are not luxuries; they are survival tools and birthrights.

To every reader holding this book: may you find healing in the broken places. May you discover softness where you once wore armor, and most of all, find your way back to yourself fully, freely, and without apology.

The journey is not behind you. It is unfolding here and now. Welcome home.

— *LaShunda Wilson, MS, LPC, NCC*

LaShunda Wilson is a licensed professional counselor and a national certified counselor with years of experience guiding women through trauma recovery, major life transitions, and personal transformation. Her career has spanned from direct care and leadership roles in foster care programs to private practice, where she combines clinical expertise with deep compassion to help clients heal, rebuild, and reclaim their voice.

INTRODUCTION

WHO HEARD HER CRY

The years I spent in the white house on the corner were the darkest and most terrifying of my life. That doesn't mean the years that followed were all good, but in that house, I came to understand the true meaning of evil. There, I learned what the devil truly looked like.

Within those walls, and through the events of that time, I came to understand the fragility of being a woman in a world that offers little to no protection. It was there that I first encountered the depths of fear and the painful truth of what it means to navigate this world unguarded.

I lived with the reality that an African American teenage mother and her baby—the most vulnerable of our society—had no support from the very systems created to protect and serve. No one intervened to stop the daily abuse we endured.

As a child, I heard people in the church talk about God's helpers and how He used them in miraculous ways. So that planted a seed in my young mind—the possible existence of an earthly protector who would be so strong and unyielding that he could shatter the walls of despair around me and rid my life of all the evil people.

During those dark times, I often dreamed of a hero who would come to rescue my mom and me. In my recurring dream, I'm sitting up on the old couch in the living room, my makeshift bed, with my knees pulled tightly to my chest. The remnants of screaming, crying, and banging lingered in the air, sharp and heavy, as if etched into the walls. The silence that followed wasn't comforting but oppressive, as though the whole world held its breath, waiting for the next eruption.

I sat peeking out the window into the hushed, shadowy street, the events of the night weighing heavily on my mind. My tiny hands clasp together as I whisper a prayer for the only thing my little heart desired: *God, please send him. Please send the Incredible Hulk.*

Yes, you read that right—the Incredible Hulk.

To my childlike mind, no one else could answer the call. He was power personified. Unstoppable. The embodiment of righteous fury. I clung to the belief that nothing angered him more than the suffering of women and children. If anyone could obliterate the evil that surrounded us, it had to be him. To me, he was more than a superhero in a comic book or on television; he was one of God's helpers. With my prayer complete, I laid down and closed my eyes.

And suddenly, as if summoned by my desperation, the house began to shake. A low, rumbling tremor turned into an earth-shattering quake, and I bolted upright, clutching the heavy blanket draped around me. The trembling grew stronger, rattling the windows and walls, until it felt like the house itself might split apart. My breath caught in my chest, and for one trembling moment, hope surged wildly inside me.

I pressed my face to the cold glass, and there he was—emerging from the darkness, larger than life, his massive frame illuminated under the flickering streetlight. His every breath was a roar, his chest heaving with fury so tangible I could feel it rippling through the air. His eyes locked on mine, and for the briefest of moments, I felt my soul exhale. Relief. Salvation. He was here, and nothing could stop him.

A big smile stretched across my face as I waved to him through the window. "You're here," I whispered, my voice shaky with relief. My hero had come. I just knew he would make everything better.

He took a powerful step toward the house, then another. But just as he reached the edge of the street, he stopped. Confusion flashed across his face as his massive fists struck something invisible in the air—a barrier I couldn't see but felt all around me every day. He hit it again, harder this time, and the sound thundered through the night.

Again and again, he pounded on the invisible shield, his roars resonating like a storm tearing through the night. "Please, Hulk!" I cried, pressing my fists against the window. "You can do it; please keep trying! God sent you!" But my words couldn't reach him, and no matter how hard he tried, the barrier refused to break.

I could see the sadness in his eyes as he realized he couldn't reach us—accepting the hard truth that his strength wasn't enough, not this time. With one final, heartbreaking roar, he turned to me. There was no anger in his eyes, just a deep sorrow that mirrored my own. It was as if he was telling me he wasn't giving up, that one day the barrier would break. Then, he slowly turned and walked back into the shadows, disappearing into the night.

The trembling ceased, and the silence returned, heavier than before. My tiny body sank onto the couch as I wrapped my arms around my knees, and tears streamed down my face. I felt so small. So trapped.

The dream was always the same—his strength, my hope, the heartbreak of that unyielding barrier. Yet even as it haunted me over the years, it carried a seed of hope. I knew how it would end, but I couldn't stop believing that one day, the shield would break. Because even in my deepest sorrow, the dream left me with one unshakable truth: I was not forgotten. Someone was fighting for me. And maybe, just maybe, I'd be free.

In real life, the Incredible Hulk never came, but I believed God would send help again. As I grew older, I began to recognize the ways He did.

The dream had planted something in me—a longing for rescue and a belief that strength greater than my own would one day break through. What I didn't realize was that God's answers wouldn't arrive as a giant green superhero. He sent helpers, protectors, and encouragers, each one becoming my own "Incredible Hulk" in disguise. Ordinary and extraordinary in their own ways, they shaped my journey.

Years later, even while outlining my debut contemporary romance novel, *Bella's Blues*, I could trace how many "Incredible Hulks" had appeared, each breaking down invisible walls bit by bit.

For me, it was my stepdad, who didn't just see the wounded pieces of me but also saw something whole and precious beneath the surface.

Who in your life has looked at you with that same unconditional love, reminding you that you are more than the pain you carry? Or maybe, like me, you've needed to learn how to accept that kind of love without questioning its genuineness.

There was my praying grandmother, whose faith was as steady and strong as the sunrise each morning. She prayed for me, her words wrapping around me like a shield. Maybe you've known someone like her—someone whose love felt like a lighthouse guiding you through the storm.

My mentor offered wisdom and encouragement that became the steady hands on the wheel steering my ship when I thought I might capsize. Do you have someone like that who sees your potential even when you can't? Maybe you are that person for someone else, gently lifting them up and reminding them of who they've always been.

And there were others: a high school friend who made me feel special, a co-worker who modeled a marriage built on faith and respect, and so many more. Each one helped tear down invisible walls that kept me feeling boxed in, untrusting, and hypervigilant. That was a survivor's way of moving through the world.

Think about the helpers in your life, the ones who broke through barriers you thought would never fall. Who are they? And how have they changed your story?

These people became my "Incredible Hulk," not in the ways I dreamed as a child, but in ways far more profound. They weren't larger than life; they were beautifully human, carrying a grounded strength and grace that had the power to heal.

I invite you to reflect on your journey. Who has been your Incredible Hulk? Or perhaps, who are you being the Incredible Hulk for today?

There was another layer to the dream I didn't grasp until much later. For years, I waited for someone else to tear down the walls, to shatter the barrier, to rescue me from the weight I was carrying. I thought deliverance would come in a booming, earth-shaking way. But healing does not always come with fanfare. Sometimes, healing is the decision to keep going—not perfect nor polished, just going.

But the real battle, the work of healing, was mine to face. No one else could fight it for me. I had to turn inward, to the one place I had avoided for so long. It was terrifying because the hardest person to confront is yourself. I kept expecting rescue to show up from somewhere else—from the hands of someone stronger, wiser, or braver than I believed myself to be. But the rescue I longed for never appeared outside; it sparked from within. Once I recognized that spark, I saw that healing was not about waiting for someone else to step in. It was about learning to answer my own cry for help.

Writing gave me the tools to begin that process. It helped me name what I had experienced, give voice to what had been buried in silence, and recognize the patterns I had lived through for far too long. In telling the truth on the page, I began to embrace the truth and release it from my spirit.

That was its own kind of awakening.

When I looked over my life's journey, three forces were constant. They were and continue to be Hope, Courage, and Grace. But they weren't just themes I wanted to write about. Hope was the flame that refused to go out even in my lowest moments. Courage was the driving force that helped me use my voice to advocate not only for myself, but for others; it helped me step into rooms and sit at tables that didn't always welcome a woman of color—a woman who looked like me. And Grace was the invitation to begin again, to keep showing up, to believe that my right to simply be and to flourish was not tied to what I had endured.

With this book, I'm not offering steps to perfection or checklists to healing—I'm offering presence. Space to exhale.

Words to help you remember that you were never meant to carry it all alone.

Reflection became that presence for me. Sometimes it found me in my car between meetings, other times in my office with the door closed for just a few quiet minutes. I learned that reflection doesn't have to be fancy or ritualistic. It can look like lighting my favorite candles—Mahogany Teakwood Intense and laundry Day—when I'm home or taking a long walk to clear the mental cobwebs when I need to breathe.

Music always sets the tone. On some days, Sade or Emeli Sandé plays softly in the background, and on others—when I need something heavier, something to match the weight I'm carrying—I turn to Adele or even my favorite rap artists. Those sounds hold space for every version of me: the woman processing, healing, or simply trying to make it through the day. Whether mellow or bold, the music becomes a kind of therapy, helping me untangle what I'm feeling and return to myself.

As I began writing these pages, I noticed how often reflection found me in those quiet spaces—journal open, candle flickering, music humming low. That mix of stillness and sound has always helped me listen to what my soul was trying to say.

Those same moments of reflection shaped the heart of this book. You'll find short sections called **Blooming Forward** throughout these pages—pauses to breathe, to notice what's stirring, to practice the art of becoming with intention. Think of them as gentle invitations to be present with your truth, one layer at a time.

And near the end, there's **The Journey to You**—a deeper reflection, like sitting with a trusted friend who asks the questions that guide you back to yourself. It's a space to write, listen, and honor how far you've come.

My hope is that by the time you finish this book, you'll have not only journeyed through my story but also created a rhythm and room for your own.

My prayer is that these pauses give you what they gave me—room to heal, to write, to remember who you are when the world grows still.

Where There Is Hope, Courage, and Grace: The Journey to Me is a reflection of these truths. It's a testament to the power of hope that anchors us, the courage that moves us, and the grace that sustains us in every season of life.

My hope is that this book becomes a source of light, a reminder that even in the darkest moments, you are not alone. Trauma, especially childhood trauma, does not define you. It leaves marks, but healing is possible when we embrace the journey and release the pain.

Each chapter of this book invites you to reflect, to rediscover your inner strength, and to find the grace that will guide you forward. You will read moments of struggle, heartbreak, and loss—but also moments of triumph, renewal, and self-discovery. Through these stories and the tools I share, I hope you'll find your anchor, your own steady ground in the middle of whatever storm you're facing. Maybe you're not sure this book will change anything. Maybe you've read a hundred self-help books and still feel stuck.

I understand. I've been there too.

But what if this isn't about changing everything? What if it's about changing one thing—your belief that you're allowed to heal?

This book isn't written from a mountaintop. It's written from the valley, from the in-between places where clarity was earned, not handed to me. If you're navigating transition or piecing yourself back together after loss, heartbreak, disappointment, or years of simply surviving, I see you.

Perhaps you've been the strong one for so long that you forgot how to ask for help. I've been there. If you're feeling an inkling of a tug to come home to yourself—even if you're scared to answer it—I wrote this with you in mind.

Early in the writing process, I made a conscious decision not to go into the graphic details of my trauma. You will find parts of my story told in truth and layered with healing, but you'll also find space for your story. Questions to sit with. Reflections to return to. And moments I pray will help you pause long enough to hear your voice again.

You may not yet know what restoration looks like, and that's okay. What matters is that you've already started. And I believe deep down, beneath the exhaustion of it all, the doubt, and the noise, you already know the way forward.

This book will not fix your life, but it will walk with you as you listen, unlearn, and bloom into the truth of who you already are.

This book is for the woman who's learned how to function while secretly breaking. For the one who shows up to work, to church, to family dinners with a smile on her face but a storm in her spirit. For the woman who has spent more time taking care of others than she's ever spent taking care of herself. And for the woman who feels like life has asked her to be strong for too long—and now, she's wondering if she even knows how to rest, to receive, or to feel joy without bracing for loss.

If that sounds like you, I want you to know something: you are not the only one.

This book is for the woman who's still piecing together parts of her story. The one who survived but hasn't yet learned what it means to live. The one with a full calendar and an aching heart, who has been silenced, overlooked, or misread, and who's finally ready to take up space in her own life again.

Maybe no one told you that healing is possible, that softness is still within reach, and that your story isn't erased. It can be reframed through the lens of grace. If no one's ever said that to you, let me be the first: you are worthy of healing. You deserve to be seen because what you carry and how you've made it this far matters.

This book is also for the younger me—the little girl who curled up on the couch with her knees pulled to her chest, hoping someone would hear her cry. The teenager who learned to wear armor just to get through the day. The woman who carried shame that was never hers to carry. I wrote this for every version of myself that ever felt forgotten, invisible, not enough, or too much. And if any part of that resonates with something you've felt, then I wrote it for you too.

Where There Is Hope, Courage, and Grace isn't a guide that promises a quick fix or a formula for pretending everything is fine. It's a companion for the real journey—the one where you stop running, stop pretending, and begin listening to the voice inside you that's been trying to rise.

It's part story, part reflection, part reminder. Each chapter invites you to read, but also to remember and revisit parts of yourself you may have tucked away—and to reclaim the pieces that still hold power.

Whether you're walking through grief, navigating transition, learning how to set boundaries, or searching for clarity after chaos, this book meets you there. It meets you in the pause between what was and what comes next. In the aching middle and the in-between.

I won't pretend that I have every answer, but I can promise you this: I'll tell the truth. Not the polished, pretty version, but the real one. The kind truth that speaks to your spirit, not just your circumstances. The truth that says, "Me too," and "Here's how." I'll show you what healing has looked like in my life—not because I've mastered it, but because I'm living it.

So if you're holding this book right now, I want you to know something beautiful is already happening—you are choosing yourself. Maybe for the first time in a long time.

Perhaps you're stepping into this season with hesitation or boldness, with your head held high. However you arrived here, however long it took, you are here. And that matters more than you know.

I wrote these pages not to fix you, but to sit beside you. To remind you that your story, with all its bends and breaks, still holds beauty. To tell you that even in your silence, you were never forgotten. And to suggest that maybe this is the chapter where things begin to shift.

The turning point doesn't come through sweeping change but through small choices to stay open—to healing, to grace, to yourself.

Carry this with you as you read. Reflection is the rhythm, healing is the melody, and self-discovery is the harmony woven through every page.

So, as we begin, I leave you with this invitation:

Let us begin the journey to you.

PART ONE: HOPE

"In order to rise from its own ashes,
a phoenix first must burn."
— *Octavia Butler*

CHAPTER 1
The Power of Hope

Have you ever felt like everything in your life was falling apart? Like the weight of the world had settled on your shoulders, and no matter which way you turned, there was no clear way out? I've been there. A few years ago, I felt like I was standing in the middle of a storm—drenched, exhausted, barely able to see a few steps ahead. I prayed for a break in the clouds, but more rain always came. More questions. More heaviness. And yet, even in those moments, something small and stubborn stayed with me: hope.

It wasn't flashy or loud, the kind you see in movies or hear in bold declarations. My hope was quieter, subtle. A gentle flutter in my chest, almost invisible but steady beneath the surface. Small, yet alive. Hope urged me forward: *There's more than this.* I didn't always know what I was hoping for. I couldn't always name it. But I longed for peace without conditions. Love that didn't hurt. Softness that didn't put me in danger. Most of all, I wanted to believe in a future bigger than the pain I had been handed. Hope didn't fix everything, but it walked with me step by step.

I clung to it as a little girl when I felt invisible in my own home or when safety was a luxury, not a guarantee. Times when grown-ups looked through my pain—or became the source of it. That's when I learned to disappear into myself. And even in that silence, something inside me dared to believe I was meant for more.

That flicker? That was hope. It spoke in moments when I was standing at the threshold of revelation, saying: *Pay attention. You're still becoming.* Hope reminded me that change was possible, even when I couldn't see the full path. That's what makes it powerful. It doesn't need a spotlight or a guarantee. It only needs a little space in your spirit, a willingness to believe something beautiful might still come from all the hurt.

I've had my share of hurt. There were days I felt like I was holding everything together with an invisible thread, trying to be strong for everybody else while falling apart inside. Mornings when I didn't want to get out of bed. Nights when I cried myself to sleep, then showed up smiling the next day. People would say, "You're so strong, nothing gets to you," and I'd want to scream, *You have no idea what it costs.* Still, hope helped me hold on to the idea of possibilities, to the truth that I was more than what had happened to me.

Almost a year before COVID, I made a career transition I had been considering for a while. Two weeks before my start date, my car broke down. Not long after, while shaping my eyebrows with a razor, I sliced my pointer finger down to the bone. Then, what I thought was a special friendship came to an abrupt end. I remember thinking, *Lord, are You preparing me for what's coming?*

The answer was yes.

I stepped into a work environment filled with dysfunction—high turnover, constant crises, layers of re-traumatizing, and overwhelming demands that made it feel like I was working around the clock. Then the world was engulfed by COVID. Because of my role, I was considered a first responder. I found myself in hospitals, correctional facilities, law enforcement offices, and client homes; business carried on as usual while the rest of the world shut down. The accumulation of everything, before and after COVID, made one truth clear: I had to make a change.

And I did.

Hope gave me the courage to step out in faith and believe my situation could shift.

Hope doesn't erase the struggle, but it reminds us we're not defined by it. There were seasons when hope felt far away, when the only thing louder than the chaos around me was the doubt inside me. I questioned everything—my purpose, my calling, whether healing was even possible.

If I'm honest, I didn't always feel like I deserved a better story. That's the part no one tells you about surviving; it wears you down in places no one else can see. Some days, you forget hope is even an option

Even so, I kept showing up. Sometimes that was all I could do—take the next breath, face the next day, and try again. Somehow, that was hope in motion. There were moments when I had no proof things would get better, no clear plan or picture-perfect ending. But I carried faith the size of a seed. I held scripture close to my heart, like Jeremiah 29:11: *"For I know the plans I have for you… plans to give you hope and a future."* I didn't always believe those words right away. Yet I repeated them, held them like a lifeline when the ache wouldn't let go, spoke them into empty rooms and tear-stained pillows, hoping they would bloom into truth. And eventually, they did.

Faith and hope held hands in me. Faith whispered, *God is still with you.* Hope answered back, *so keep going.* There's a kind of hope that grows quietly, like pressing down where no one can see, creating space for life to grow even in broken soil.

I think back to the people who watered those roots in me: my grandmother and her unwavering prayers, a mentor who spoke life into me when I couldn't see myself clearly, and a friend who told me, *"You're not broken; you're just carrying too much."* Those words mattered. Those prayers mattered. Love like that becomes soil where hope can breathe.

Hope grows in the presence of love—the real kind. The kind that doesn't try to fix you but says, *you don't have to carry this alone.* If no one has said that to you lately, or maybe ever, let me say it now: you don't have to carry it alone. You were never meant to. You are allowed to lean on others. You may not feel ready to voice it aloud, but deep within, hope is already speaking. It can surface in ways you don't expect: tears that come without warning, a long-held breath you finally release, a small act of care that feels insignificant to others but sacred to you, or even a quiet yearning for something more.

That longing, however fragile, is hope. Alive and present within you.

This journey isn't about pretending everything is fine. It's about trusting that even in the messy, not-okay moments, something meaningful is unfolding. Healing is taking root, your spirit is stretching, and the story of your life is opening in new ways. You are in motion, and you are becoming.

If you've ever found yourself caught between despair and desire, between silence and survival, that is where healing begins. Not when everything makes sense, but when you stop pretending and allow truth to take up space. Sometimes that truth is as simple as saying, *I don't know what's next, but I know I want more than this.*

Hope doesn't rewrite what happened, but it gives you the courage to write what comes next. Becoming rarely begins with fixing what feels broken; more often, it starts with recognizing what has always remained whole.

As I close this chapter, I think about how hope has always been less about knowing the way and more about daring to keep walking. It never erased my storms, but it reminded me I was not defined by them. That steady thread of belief held me together long enough to begin again.

Beginning again didn't happen overnight. It started when I stopped looking outside myself for permission to heal. When I turned inward—messy, uncertain, and raw—and began asking honest questions: *Who am I now? What parts of me are waiting to be seen? What am I carrying that no longer belongs?*

With hope as my compass, I stepped into deeper work—the inward healing work. Healing doesn't just live in the light; it begins in the shadows, where truth breathes and silence finally speaks.

In the seasons when everything feels like it's falling apart, that is where courage often begins. That is where hope grows. Every return to yourself is a step forward. And as you move ahead, remember this: the journey of becoming doesn't end here. Embracing hope and honoring your story is preparing you for more—a life aligned with purpose, carried out with intention.

BLOOMING FORWARD

Hope isn't always a feeling that sweeps in with certainty; sometimes it's a quiet decision you make while standing in uncertainty. It's the moment you choose to keep moving, even when the pain hasn't lifted and the answers haven't yet arrived. That choice alone is powerful, because it opens the door to possibility. Hope does not demand guarantees—it invites you to believe you are worthy of gentleness, of something more than what you've endured. Even if the words never leave your lips, the desire itself is enough to begin.

There is resilience in honoring tender beginnings, in giving weight to the parts of yourself that have carried too much. You don't have to prove readiness or earn worthiness. Sometimes the bravest act is simply to say, *I'm here, and I want to live differently.* Hope lives inside that admission. It takes root in your honesty, in your willingness to lean toward something greater, even if the growth feels slow.

As poet Morgan Harper Nichols once wrote, *"Perhaps the reason you are drawn to the ocean is because it reminds you: you have come this far, and you are still becoming."* Hope doesn't still the tide, but it helps you breathe through it. Scripture reminds us that hope is not fragile or fleeting, but a gift from God. Romans 15:13 (NIV) declares, *"May the God of hope fill you with all joy and peace as you trust in him, so that you may overflow with hope by the power of the Holy Spirit."* This isn't about perfect faith; it's about trusting in motion, believing the same God who met you in your most vulnerable moments is still guiding you forward.

Take a moment today to honor this truth. Write a note to the version of yourself who kept going when she longed to give up. Thank her. Remind her that faithfulness was enough, even when fear was loud. Then write a note to the version of you who is still unfolding—what would it mean to believe she is already enough? What would it look like to let kindness shape her next step?

Let that be your practice today: not performing healing, but returning to it with gentleness. You don't have to chase hope; you make space for it when you speak truthfully, when you treat yourself with compassion. That's where hope takes root. Every return is a step forward.

CHAPTER 2
Looking Inward: Where it all Begins

The hardest part about looking inward is realizing how long you've been searching everywhere else. I had spent much of my life in survival mode—smiling when I wanted to cry, adapting to whatever room I walked into, and performing the version of myself I thought others expected: the "Strong Black Woman." But underneath that mask was someone I barely recognized, a woman worn down physically and emotionally, so consumed with carrying other people's burdens that she had forgotten where she existed apart from their needs.

Eventually, life forced me to stop. Stress from my job collided with the weight of everything else I'd been carrying, and my body made it clear that I couldn't keep pushing without consequence. My struggles with anemia, PCOS, and fibroids flared worse than ever, and a new layer of anxiety-like symptoms appeared. I was exhausted, sleep-deprived, and heavier than I had ever been. Triggers I had ignored for years were demanding attention. The reflection in the mirror felt like a stranger's face, and I was certain something inside me was unraveling.

I went from one doctor's office to another—hematologist, gynecologist, primary care—grasping for answers. While their treatments offered some relief, the unease inside me didn't go away. One day, my mom said, "Victoria, you are not happy."

And you know what? I wasn't happy.

Saying it out loud made me pause in a way I hadn't before. *Hearing myself admit it out loud changed everything.* It became the pivot point that pushed me to take an honest inventory of my life—my career, associations, relationships, everything—and admit I wasn't where I wanted to be. That moment shifted everything. I stopped waiting for someone else to fix my circumstances or provide the remedy. I realized this part of the work—this deep, tender, unsettling work—was mine to do.

For the first time, I truly stopped and took stock of where I was and what I wanted for my future. I stopped waiting for outside forces to fix my life or offer remedies. I realized this part of the healing was mine to do.

Looking inward meant telling the truth about what hurt, about what I had buried, and about who I had become in the name of survival. It meant sitting with the parts of me I had tried to silence: the anger, fear, exhaustion, the dreams I had abandoned, and the boundaries I had allowed others to cross without checking them appropriately. It meant listening to the younger version of myself, the one who never had the chance to speak.

Looking inward is a hard process, but it is essential. When you truly listen to yourself, you begin to remember. You remember what you once hoped for before the world tried to define you. You remember the strength it took just to make it this far. And you realize that survival is not the same as living, and there is more waiting for you.

For a long time, I thought healing was something I could schedule. If I read enough books, prayed enough prayers, attended enough conferences, and gathered enough quotes, then maybe I would finally arrive at the version of me I felt was missing. I imagined there was a finish line—some polished, perfect self waiting on the other side.

But looking inward showed me a different truth: healing is not a destination. It is a relationship with yourself, your past, and your process. It unfolds in layers, each one revealing something new to face or embrace.

There were parts of me I felt proud to confront—my ambition, my heart, the way I showed up for people. But there were other parts that were harder to sit with. I carried the weight of my childhood trauma as if it were mine alone. I struggled to give love unconditionally without fearing it wouldn't be returned. I silenced myself in rooms where my voice belonged because I sensed it might not matter.

Those parts weren't easy to face, but they were teaching me something. They pointed to the places where I had learned to survive by masking. Out of that realization, I began living by a new principle I call being "on the record." Whether or not my voice will be heard, no matter how the room feels, I make sure it is on the record. That means I speak my truth because it holds value to me, and once I release it, I no longer have to carry the weight of silence.

Maya Angelou once wrote, *"There's no greater agony than bearing an untold story inside you."* I have learned that not sharing how you truly feel in the moment—in the meetings you attend, at the tables you've been invited to, or even at the ones you've created—brings its own kind of agony. Staying silent to keep the peace only deepens the ache.

What I have come to understand is that we don't build these patterns for no reason. Every defense mechanism, every wall I constructed, every time I chose silence over truth—it was all rooted in protection. The little girl in me did what she had to do to feel safe, and I honor her for that. She helped me survive.

But the woman I am now? She has permission to live differently.

Looking inward helped me realize I never needed to be "fixed," because I was never broken. I am a layered person with a complex history, and those layers carry stories. Some are painful, some are beautiful, and some are still unfolding.

One of the hardest layers to face was the one wrapped in shame. I carried shame about what had been done to me and about the choices I made when I wasn't prepared. It is easy to condemn ourselves for the seasons when we didn't know better. But how can we fault ourselves for doing what we thought we had to do to survive?

My healing began when I started speaking to myself with the same compassion I so easily gave to others. When I practiced positive self-talk, stopped rushing past my sadness, and treated my emotions as invitations instead of inconveniences, I began to feel whole. Not perfect—whole.

We are often our own harshest critics. I used to measure myself by what I had not accomplished, instead of recognizing how much I had already overcome. Statistically, I was expected to be among the overlooked, the have-nots. Yet here I was, standing, surviving, and in many ways thriving, even when the world had counted me out.

There is a softness that comes with inner work—the tender shift when you realize you no longer have to brace yourself for every moment. The clarity that I don't have to hustle the masses to be seen. Who I am, right now, is worthy of love, rest, joy, and truth.

Let me be honest—sometimes I still forget that. I catch myself trying to prove that something good has to come from everything I've faced. I notice when I slip back into striving, over-explaining, or staying silent when I should speak. But now, instead of shaming myself, I notice it with gentleness. I come back to myself. I realize I'm not trying to prove myself to the outside world; I'm trying to prove something to me. By holding that belief, I trust the right people will notice. The right doors will open, and more importantly, I see myself clearly. I'm no longer chasing applause; I'm honoring alignment.

That is what looking inward teaches: how to return to yourself, not with judgment but with love.

Here's the truth: looking inward doesn't guarantee instant clarity. It doesn't mean you'll wake up tomorrow with everything figured out. But it does give you something priceless: awareness. And once you become aware, you cannot unsee.

It's like pulling out that dress you try on every few months, hoping it will finally fit differently—only to find the same soft rolls are still there, holding on like soft-plump baby jaws. Awareness works the same way. You begin to notice what no longer fits. You catch the untruths you used to believe, the habits that once felt natural, the ways you abandoned yourself without realizing it. And slowly, you begin craving honesty in a new way.

For me to grow and heal, I had to turn inward—the very place I had avoided for so long. It was frightening, because sometimes the hardest work is facing yourself.

Looking inward meant confronting the fragile parts of me I had buried deep. It meant examining the shattered pieces of my heart one by one and trusting—truly believing—that healing was possible, even when it felt out of reach.

In the introduction, I shared my recurring dream of the Incredible Hulk. In the dream, he could not break the barrier that stood between us. But I discovered that I could. Not all at once, and not without help, but brick by brick, with each small act of courage, I began to tear it down.

That is where the real journey begins—not when someone else rescues you, but when you decide to face what is inside. To sit with the pain, to feel the weight of it, and then to rise. To rise and take the first step toward healing.

You don't need to be fully healed to love yourself or to accept the person staring back at you in the mirror. You don't need to be fearless to move forward. What you need is honesty, compassion, and a willingness to try.

Looking inward isn't only about naming what hurts; it's also about reclaiming what has been hidden—your voice, your strength, your truth. Self-awareness opens the door. And once you truly begin to see yourself, something else happens too: you start to believe that healing is possible, that change is within reach, and that you are worthy of more. That belief is where transformation takes root.

In this chapter, we embraced the boldness it takes to tell the truth, to ask questions with kindness, and to honor our own needs without guilt. These are not small acts—they carry power. The next chapter invites us into a new rhythm: one where belief in our potential grows stronger than doubt. We are not just uncovering what hurt; we are stepping into what is possible. Let's explore what it means to believe, even before we see.

BLOOMING FORWARD

There is something deeply human and healing about being willing or having the courage to look inward and stay a while. Not to dissect yourself until you are weary or try to fix every flaw you think you see, but to witness the truth of who you are and what you've carried. Before the growth, clarity, or breakthrough... there's the noticing. The slow unfolding of your own story in front of you. It's okay if that unfolding feels tender. You're not doing it wrong just because it still hurts. That willingness to turn inward is not small—it's transformational.

Healing begins with the smallest act of courage, naming what you feel without filtering it. Other times, it starts when you see yourself clearly not as broken, but as someone who has lived, endured, stretched, and survived. You are not a problem to be solved. You are a person to be understood. And when you turn that understanding inward—when you stop abandoning yourself in the name of performance or peacekeeping—you begin to reclaim parts of you that were never really lost, only hidden until you were ready to be seen again.

It may feel tender, even raw, to face yourself honestly, but that tenderness is not weakness; it's the soil where new growth takes root. Every time you pause to honor what you feel instead of rushing past it, you are reclaiming yourself. You are saying, *I matter too.*

There will be days when looking inward feels heavy, when it seems easier to reach for distractions or to keep hiding, numbing your feelings, or trying to escape. But if you stay with yourself, even for a little while, you'll discover something profound: awareness. And awareness opens doors. It shows you not only what has wounded you, but what has kept you alive. It reveals the parts of you that were never broken, only waiting to be remembered.

As Cheryl Strayed once wrote, *"You don't have a right to the cards you believe you should have been dealt. You have an obligation to play the hell out of the ones you're holding."* Scripture echoes this invitation: *"See, I am doing a new thing! Now it springs up; do you not perceive it? I am making a way in the wilderness and streams in the wasteland"* (Isaiah 43:19, NIV). God reminds us that even when we feel stuck or worn down, newness is being formed in us.

So today, ask yourself gently: *What part of me have I ignored to keep going? What truth have I softened to make others comfortable? What do I need—not tomorrow, not next year, but right now?* These questions are not demands. They are invitations. And every time you answer them honestly, you take one more step toward becoming.

Looking inward is not about perfection. It's about presence. The more present you become with your own soul, the more space you create for healing to grow. You are not too late, and you are not too much. You are arriving. And each time you choose to look inward with honesty and love, you are blooming forward.

CHAPTER 3

Believing in Possibilities

It's hard to believe in possibilities when you've been conditioned to expect disappointment. Every time you let your hopes rise, life seemed to knock them back down. You learned not to get too excited, simply to avoid the ache of being let down again. Dreams became "unrealistic," not because they truly were, but because it felt safer to call them that. I know that mindset well; I lived in it for years. I told myself I was just being practical, that I was "keeping it real."

Beneath that, I was guarded, vulnerable, and full of doubt. Guarded, because wanting something with my whole heart always carried the risk of watching it slip away. Vulnerable, because naming a dream felt like opening myself up to rejection. Doubtful, because society has drilled into us the idea that we should be grateful for what we have—and that wanting more is somehow wrong. Especially in certain communities, where survival often gets mistaken for contentment.

So, I settled. Not just in relationships or jobs, but in how I imagined my future. By most standards, my life looked fine. But underneath, a voice kept rising: There has to be more than this. That voice was right. Believing in possibility doesn't erase fear—it means hope gets a chance to speak louder, even for a moment. It means allowing yourself to imagine that something good could still happen, that it isn't too late.

The truth is, most of us don't stop dreaming because we lose interest. We stop because we're tired—tired of disappointment, of explaining our vision to people who don't understand, of pretending not to care when we care deeply.

But possibility doesn't demand flawless timing—it asks for willingness. You don't need the blueprint or the entire plan mapped out. You only need the courage to say, I'm open. For years, I thought dreams came with an expiration date—that if they hadn't happened by a certain age, they weren't meant for me. I watched others moving forward, leveling up, glowing in ways I longed for, while I felt stuck in a holding pattern, circling possibilities I didn't think I'd ever reach.

Here's what I've come to understand: delay doesn't equal denial. What looked like stagnation often turned out to be preparation. Looking back, I see those years were laying a foundation. Like any lasting structure, the foundation matters most; without it, nothing built on top can stand or survive shifting seasons.

Believing in possibility meant redefining success—not by timelines or titles, but by alignment. Did it bring me alive? Did it honor who I was becoming? Was it rooted in truth or just survival? These became the questions I started asking. Because settling no longer felt safe, it felt like suffocation.

One of the first times I dared to say yes to possibility was when I finally let myself admit, *I want more*—without shame. Not more stuff or status, but more peace, connection, genuine moments, and alignment between who I was and how I lived. It began as soft declarations scribbled in my journal and spoken during late-night drives, but even those quiet confessions shifted something inside me. Because possibility begins the second we stop trying to fit a story that was never ours to carry.

I used to think dreaming big meant being unrealistic. Now I see it differently: dreaming big is remembering who you were before life taught you to doubt yourself. It's reclaiming the version of you who dared to believe before heartbreak, betrayal, and shame tried to silence that voice.

The first step?

It was giving myself space to be seen, even by me. For me, that meant rebuilding the foundation for entrepreneurship and reigniting my author journey, even when I hadn't written in a while. It meant saying yes to rooms I didn't think I belonged in. It meant receiving compliments without immediately deflecting them.

Possibility often begins in the smallest of moments—in the split-second choices that whisper, *I believe something good can still come from this.*

I remember being invited to speak at an event, and my first instinct was to say no. Not because I lacked the desire, but because I didn't feel ready. I thought of every reason I may not be the right person—too quiet, not engaging enough, not polished enough. I wondered if they had chosen the wrong person.

Then came a different question, one that cut through the noise: *What if they didn't?*

Imposter syndrome almost convinced me to decline, but that same small voice I had ignored for years urged me to believe something different. So, I said yes.

Standing there that day, I realized the only barrier between me and that moment was the story I had been telling myself. Possibility had always been waiting. I just had to stop disqualifying myself from it.

It's amazing how one shift in language can unlock entirely new realities—it gave me curiosity. And curiosity became the spark of momentum.

I remember sitting on the couch one evening, Sade playing low in the background, a blank journal open on my lap. I felt caught between the weight of what was and the pull of what could be. The questions came first, tentative but alive: *What if I could? What if finishing this is still possible? What if I'm not behind, but being prepared for more?* At first, those questions were gentle stirrings of curiosity, but the more I wrote, the more they began to sound like declarations. I wasn't only asking anymore—I was daring to believe.

Believing in possibility didn't mean I had everything figured out; it meant I was willing to take one step closer to myself, authentically. That shift didn't happen all at once, but it carried a quiet authority. What began as doubt-tinged wondering became a seed of conviction. Curiosity had opened the door, but claiming kept me walking through it.

Belief doesn't always come with confidence. Sometimes it begins as a fragile question: *Is this really the only story I can tell myself?* From there comes the courage to imagine a different one. We build momentum not by bulldozing fear but by allowing another voice to speak up; the voice that says, *I might be scared, but I'm still willing. I might not know the path, but I can take one small step.*

That's what I began doing: saying yes to one conversation I would've avoided, one opportunity I once would've declined, one truth I was finally brave enough to speak. The narrative began to turn.

When you allow yourself to believe, your body moves differently. Your spirit rises. You stop waiting for evidence and start becoming it. If you've ever taken one step toward something that scared you, or dared to hope with trembling hands, you're already doing it. You're already blooming.

Some days, believing feels like defiance—especially when life keeps handing you reason after reason to give up: another closed door, another unanswered prayer, another goodbye you didn't want. I used to think those obstacles meant I had failed, that maybe I didn't believe hard enough. But what if none of that is true? What if the dream takes longer, not because you're lacking or being punished, but because you're being strengthened for it? What if your "not yet" is fertile ground?

Possibility doesn't always arrive with sparkles. Sometimes it shows up disguised as detours, disappointments, or long stretches of waiting that shape us in way we don't see until later. I think back to one of my lowest seasons. I was emotionally drained, spiritually weary, and financially stretched thin. I sat in my car outside a job I had a love–hate relationship with, tears streaming down my face. Staying felt unbearable, yet the uncertainty of leaving unsettled me just as much.

In that moment, I whispered a prayer: *God, if there's more for me, show me.* I wasn't asking for fireworks or some dramatic sign. I just needed a glimpse of something to hold on to, a reminder that possibility hadn't abandoned me. And as I prayed, I added one more plea: *Help me recognize it when it comes—even if it doesn't look like what I expect.*

The instant you say, *I want more,* the shift begins. It doesn't always look like launching something big. Sometimes it's finishing what you left half-done on the shelf. Sometimes it's booking that therapy appointment or finally setting a boundary. Other times, it's as simple as speaking your truth out loud—or letting yourself rest without guilt.

Every one of those choices is a seed. Each small yes declares: *I believe my life can expand beyond this version.* And I know—it's hard, especially when no one is clapping yet. When the world tells you to just be grateful, even if what you have is wearing you down. But here's the truth: you are allowed to want more. Not because you're greedy or ungrateful, but because something in you knows the story isn't finished yet.

Sometimes the bravest thing you can do is name what you want. Not just the survival goals, but the longings that live deep in your spirit—the ones that make your voice shake. The ones you've hidden because you feared they were too much. For a long time, I wrestled with the idea that wanting more meant I wasn't grateful enough. But I've learned that gratitude and desire can live side by side. You can honor what you have while still believing in what's next.

Believing doesn't mean you never doubt; it means you move anyway. You speak life, even when your voice wavers. You ask. You apply. You try again because something inside you refuses to give up. That spark—that steady insistence on more—is the seed of transformation.

And here's what I've discovered: belief often begins where proof runs out.

You might not see the evidence yet, but you take a step forward anyway, planting in soil no one else can see. That doesn't make it any less real. Some of my most meaningful changes came when I stopped demanding certainty and started trusting the unseen. Momentum didn't come all at once—it gathered slowly, through small yeses, everyday courage, and decisions that didn't look spectacular but built strength over time.

That's when life began to move—not perfectly, but powerfully. And here's the gift in it: this, too, is part of your becoming story. You don't have to wait until the path is clear or the applause comes. Belief is enough to keep you rising, one step at a time.

This chapter invites you to believe again—not just in the possibility of healing or growth, but in your belonging within it. As we move forward, we'll explore what it means to hold on to light in the midst of shadows because healing isn't always a straight line. And even in the darkest stretches, you were never truly alone.

BLOOMING FORWARD

Believing again isn't always about grand leaps or polished affirmations. Sometimes it looks like sitting with yourself, admitting what you long for, and refusing to abandon that desire. The power isn't in having all the answers—it's in allowing yourself to want, even when you don't yet know how it will unfold. Possibility shows up not only in victories, but in the brave act of remaining open when uncertainty tempts you to close off. There is something profoundly human about continuing to imagine more for yourself, even when the world tells you to settle.

You are allowed to want beauty after loss. You are allowed to carry hope in difficult seasons and to keep your dreams alive even when the path is unclear. Desire doesn't make you ungrateful; it makes you alive. The soul expands in the space between what has been and what might yet be. Though that stretching may ache, it plants resilience in you—resilience that will not easily be shaken. Faith that grows in uncertainty often becomes the strongest kind.

Poet Andrea Gibson once wrote, "Your heartbeat is a rhythm of hope drumming its way back to you." That rhythm may feel faint at times, but it is steady. It's the part of you that continues to show up, continues to try, continues to murmur *maybe* when your mind insists it's too late. And God, who knows the deepest corners of your heart, honors that spark. Romans 4:18 (NIV) says of Abraham, "Against all hope, Abraham in hope believed…" Choosing to believe without visible proof does more than change circumstances—it transforms you.

So pause for a moment. Ask yourself: What would it mean to believe with gentleness instead of pressure? What if you held space for your dream without rushing it into existence? Write it down, not only what you hope to accomplish, but how you want to feel when it arrives. Let belief be the soil, not the performance.

Faith doesn't need to be forced. It grows through small acts of trust—resting when your body asks, speaking truth even when your voice is unsteady, leaving room in your day to breathe and tell yourself, *I still want this.* That wanting is not weakness; it is proof that your story is still unfolding.

Your belief doesn't have to look like anyone else's. It just has to be honest. Even if you're figuring it out step by step. Even if you're afraid. Because some of the most life-altering shifts don't start with certainty; they begin with the deliberate, courageous choice to believe again anyway.

CHAPTER 4
Overcoming Darkness

There are parts of my story I don't like to revisit. Not out of shame, but because they cost me something. There's grief in remembering how much I had to carry—how young I was when I learned to scan a room for exits, to hold my breath in moments that should have felt safe. I became a master of pretending because pretending felt safer than telling the truth.

You learn to survive by hiding parts of yourself, by becoming invisible in the moments that feel most dangerous. For me, that meant smiling when I wanted to scream, shrinking so I wouldn't be noticed, reading emotions like survival cues, and shifting who I was to avoid conflict. It became second nature, yet it never stopped hurting. Each time I swallowed my truth, I lost a piece of myself. Back then, silence felt safer than honesty.

Darkness takes many forms—trauma or the silence that follows. Sometimes it's the way people see you survive and call it strength, yet they never see the tears that fall when the lights go out. There's a strange loneliness in being praised for surviving what no one truly understands. People celebrate your composure and grace under pressure, but they don't see the toll it takes behind closed doors. The sleepless nights become a constant struggle between staying silent and expressing your truth. The world praises your resilience when what you really long for is rest. You want softness, someone to see beyond the surface and say, "You don't have to be strong today."

I didn't choose the pain I went through, but I chose what to do with it. That choice didn't come easily. For years, I avoided naming it. I thought speaking it aloud would give it power. But I learned this: what we refuse to face continues to hold us, not because it's stronger than us, but because we haven't taken time to understand what it has cost us.

There's a kind of exhaustion that settles deep in your bones when you've carried unspoken trauma. On the outside, you may appear fine, but inwardly, the weight never allows you to rest. Eventually, even the best mask begins to slip. The ache becomes too overwhelming to ignore, and you start to question whether mere survival is enough—if you were meant for more than just getting by.

The darkness I lived through wasn't a single chapter; it was a season that stretched on longer than I could have imagined. I've faced betrayal that shattered trust, been touched without consent, and walked through life with a trauma-shaped lens, flinching at kindness because I wasn't sure it was real.

Those experiences left marks—not always visible, but deeply embedded in how I moved through the world. I questioned people's intentions, even the kind ones. I hesitated before sharing simple truths. I second-guessed joy because I had learned that pain often followed. I wasn't just carrying memories; I was carrying the lessons those moments taught me: that safety was fleeting, trust was dangerous, and so-called love could wound.

I didn't realize how much of my childhood trauma still lived inside me until I started working in that high-stress job. That's when memories I had tucked away in the back of my mind began to surface. At one point, one of my "Me Too" people started stalking me on social media. Because I had blocked so much out, I only remembered his childhood name, so I didn't recognize him by the name on the profile. The picture wasn't him either. After blocking one account, another request would come. Then another. Eventually, I looked at the profile—and there it was. He had taken pictures from my page and posted them as if they were his, as if he were part of those moments. I felt sick. I started deleting my photos, stopped posting pictures of myself, and limited what I shared to quotes and holiday posts. It felt like being re-violated, a shadow of something I thought I had escaped. I eventually confided in someone I trusted and, little by little, began to reclaim my space. I started taking pictures again. I started showing up.

Another turning point came when I finally told my mother what happened to me as a child. I softened the story, protecting the parts of her that I knew were fragile. I didn't want her to be blindsided if the truth surfaced elsewhere. Speaking those words out loud, even in a gentler form, still felt like a release—a complicated one—but necessary.

The body remembers every wound, whether physical, emotional, or spiritual. Eventually, my silence became sickness. I felt exhausted in every way a person could be. Still, I kept moving, because that's what I had always done. I knew how to push through, how to compartmentalize. What I didn't know was how to rest.

For most of my life, I believed that stopping meant losing ground. That showing weakness meant defeat. That belief still lingers at times, but I've learned to pair it with rest, honest self-talk, and stillness. The thing about darkness is that it can be suffocating, but it also reveals the strength of your light. It doesn't erase it—it shows you where it's needed most. When the roles, the image, and the constant striving fall away, what remains is truth. What remains is the light you didn't know had survived.

I reached a point when I was bone-tired, soul-weary—the kind of tired that sleep cannot soothe. I was drowning in unspoken grief and truths I hadn't admitted. I wondered, "Is this what the rest of life will feel like?" I had spent so much time being what others needed that I'd forgotten what I needed. Yet something inside me refused to let go. That was the moment I knew survival wasn't enough anymore. I needed something deeper. That realization marked the beginning of healing. It was the first time I stopped bracing for the past and began reaching for peace.

Healing doesn't happen in a straight line. It happens in spirals. You think you've made peace until something brings it back. Letting go feels complete until someone touches a wound you forgot was open. Forgiveness seems sure until old memories resurface, clenched and raw. Still, each time I faced it without turning away, I took some of my power back—not all at once, but piece by piece.

Some of the people who hurt me never apologized. For a while, I tried to make their actions make sense. Eventually, I stopped excusing what had no excuse and stopped softening the truth to make it easier for others to hear. I began validating myself: Yes, it happened. Yes, it hurt. Yes, I deserved better. And no, it wasn't my fault.

Healing didn't depend on everyone else acknowledging the harm; it depended on me no longer pretending it didn't matter. I could release the guilt and shed the shame that never belonged to me, dismissing the false belief that pain has to look pretty to be taken seriously. Some pain is jagged, raw, still bleeding—and even then, it deserves to be heard.

Darkness is messy, heavy, and honest. And honesty is where healing begins. It isn't curated or polished; it's raw and real—the kind that demands you stop pretending everything is fine. When the walls you've built start to crumble, what's left isn't weakness. It's the truth of who you are beneath the weight of what you've carried. That truth becomes the first light guiding you back to yourself.

One of the most powerful steps I took was telling the truth—first to myself. I stopped editing my memories, minimizing the damage, and pretending I was okay because the world expected it. In doing so, I found my voice. Not the version shaped by expectation, but the one buried beneath survival—the one that still believed in softness, the one that knew how to dream. That, right there, is what healing looks like in motion.

I claimed my story, not to become someone new, but to return to who I was before the world convinced me I had to earn my worth.

Overcoming darkness doesn't mean the pain disappears. It means learning how to carry light again. You stop waiting for a perfect ending and start honoring the fact that you're still here—breathing, choosing, becoming.

Healing takes time. It's rarely neat or linear. But each time you show up for yourself, you rewrite the story. You reclaim your light as you continue to rise.

Each time I revisit my story, I find new meaning in what I survived and a deeper understanding of what it means to still be here. Healing didn't erase the pain, but it taught me how to live with both ache and awe—to see survival as the beginning of something new. In the next chapter, I'll share one of the hardest moments of my life, a time when the weight of it all nearly silenced me completely. But even then, even in that darkness, something within me held on.

BLOOMING FORWARD

There's a moment in every healing journey when silence begins to shift—not always through words, but through awareness. You stop swallowing your grief and start acknowledging it. You stop editing the past to make it easier to carry, and you begin to tell the truth with clarity and compassion. You're not doing it to stay stuck or to seek validation; you're doing it to be free. Naming your pain doesn't mean weakness—it means you feel safe enough to stop hiding. And that safety allows healing to take root.

You don't need to wear a mask to be seen. You don't have to soften your truth or silence your story to make others comfortable. The power of your voice comes not from pretense, but from honesty. When you stand as you are, without apology or disguise, you remind yourself and others that authenticity carries its own kind of strength. And that version of you? She deserves tenderness that holds her without condition, that sees her fully and stays.

There is no weakness in needing time, nor shame in grieving the pieces of yourself you had to set aside just to get through the day. You are not broken; you are healing in layers. Even if no one else saw the depth of what you carried, God did. "Record my misery; list my tears on your scroll—are they not in your record?" (Psalm 56:8, NIV). Every tear, every night you felt invisible, none of it was forgotten.

As you peel back the layers of survival, you might feel uncertain, tender, open in ways you haven't in years. But that's where restoration begins—not in having it all together, but in being willing to feel again. To remember that your softness isn't a flaw; it's part of your strength. This isn't about going back to who you were before the pain. It's about becoming more fully who you've always been underneath it.

Poet Nikita Gill wrote, "Some days, I am more fire than girl, and some days I am more girl than fire. But both days, I am still burning." That's the truth of healing. It isn't always steady. Some days you'll feel brave; other days, heavy. But even when your light flickers low, it hasn't gone out. You are still here, still rising, still reclaiming the pieces of yourself that were never meant to stay hidden.

This week, let your healing be gentle. Don't rush to be okay. Sit with the version of you who kept going when it was hardest. Say to her: I see you. You weren't imagining it. You deserved better. And you don't have to carry this alone anymore. Lay it down—not to forget, but to breathe again. You are not defined by the darkness. You are defined by your decision to heal anyway.

CHAPTER 5

Still Here

I don't make it a habit of dwelling on the events of my childhood. But there are times they creep up on me, uninvited. A few years ago, I was watching the Tyler Perry movie *I Can Do Bad All By Myself*. There's a scene between Madea and Jennifer—April's niece—where Jennifer breaks down and says she's tired of dealing with things a child shouldn't have to deal with. I felt tears roll down my face before I even realized I was crying. That scene transported me, instantly and viscerally, back to being a little girl who had already carried far too much.

At that age, I didn't have the language for depression. I didn't know what trauma was or how it affects the body and mind. I just knew the ache, the weight of it all, and wanted the suffering to stop.

There's something incredibly disorienting about holding that much pain without the vocabulary or tools to make sense of it. I wasn't being dramatic or rebellious; I was exhausted. That exhaustion wasn't something a nap could cure, or a toy could distract me from. It ran deeper, worn into the fabric of my small, tender frame.

I had recently been to the doctor for an ear infection and was prescribed antibiotics. That night, I said a prayer, asking God to forgive me. I'd been taught that suicide was a sin. I didn't want to go to hell. I was a good kid, a good person. But I was about to do something I believed might send me away from God forever. And that terrified me.

I still remember the fear that came with that prayer—not of dying, but of disappointing God.

Still, I did it. I took the bottle of antibiotics and what was left in a container of over-the-counter pain medicine. I don't remember falling asleep. But I remember waking up; it was just after 11 a.m., way later than I usually slept on a Saturday, especially when a bowl of cereal and cartoons were waiting for me. But that day, I didn't rush to the TV.

I just lay there. Still. Breathing. Confused. Because I wasn't supposed to wake up.

And yet... I did. I cried, not tears of joy, but of confusion, from the ache of still being here—of needing to survive another day in a life I hadn't asked for. I was tired. Still small. Still needing something I didn't have the words for. But beneath the ache, something else stirred. An unspoken knowing I couldn't explain. God hadn't let me go. Not out of punishment, but because something in me continued to matter.

There was still breath left to give.

I didn't tell anyone what I had done. Not for years. I carried that morning like a secret seed, buried deep, waiting to bloom when I was ready to understand it. I didn't revisit it often, but it never left me. It became part of my inner landscape, a lasting marker of both pain and resilience. It lived in my silence—in the way I overachieved and smiled, even when I was breaking inside.

And even then, I didn't fully grasp the depth of that moment.

Back then, I thought waking up meant I had to be stronger, do more, be better, earn the life I had been "given back." But now I know it meant something much simpler and far more life-affirming: *keep going.* That morning didn't come with fireworks or revelations, but with the uncomfortable awareness that I was still alive.

That morning has become a spiritual landmark for me. A perceptual turning point because I survived. Over the years, I've come to understand that surviving wasn't a failure of my plan; it was a fulfillment of my purpose. I realized I wasn't being punished by God for trying to end my pain. I was preserved—not to perform or prove anything, but to live. To begin again, even in the midst of brokenness.

At the time, I didn't have the tools to process what I'd done. I didn't know that children can experience complex trauma that accumulates like layers—trauma that begins long before they have the vocabulary to explain it. I didn't know that what I had carried was too heavy for anyone, let alone a child. I just knew I was tired. I had absorbed the weight of things far beyond my years and was expected to hold it all with grace. But grace without relief becomes a burden. And that burden almost took me out.

Now, with years behind me and healing in my hands, I look back at that morning not just with sorrow, but with reverence. It wasn't my ending, it was my beginning. The beginning of a journey I didn't choose, but one I've grown to honor. A journey that's been messy, nonlinear, and often hard to name.

But one that has shaped me in ways I'm only now beginning to understand.

There's a reason I'm still here. And that reason isn't because I've done everything right or been the strongest or most faithful. It's because God never let go—even when I couldn't see beyond my circumstances or believed the lie that being tired meant I was weak. Even in moments of despair, when I thought the world would be better off without me, God stayed.

I am not ashamed of that night. I'm not proud of it either. But I hold it tenderly. Because it reminds me that survival, at its core, is endurance with a pulse. When the darkness tried to take me out, the light in me—no matter how faint, was never extinguished.

That morning, I didn't rise with a plan. I didn't wake up with hope. I just woke up. But waking up planted something, and I've been watering it ever since.

There's a deep kind of courage in naming what almost broke you and an even deeper one in choosing to live beyond it. That morning, I didn't rise with understanding, but I rose. Every day since has been part of the unfolding. Healing didn't erase the ache, but it gave me language and foundation. It reminded me that my story, however heavy, is still being written. And so is yours.

The truth about trauma is that it doesn't always end with one event; it often keeps resonating in the years that follow. In those moments when you wonder if anyone will ever see beneath your strength, when you feel pressed to explain what should never need justification. Surviving that day wasn't only about staying alive; it was about something within me refusing to let go.

I haven't returned to that night in the same way I lived it as a child, because I am no longer that little girl without language, safety, or a voice. The woman I am now carries emotional intelligence, hard-won self-awareness, and a support system I trust with my truth. The memory of that morning remains a marker on my journey—not a place I live in, but a reminder of where I've come from and what I've learned to hold with care. It taught me that strength isn't always loud or unshaken. Sometimes it's the decision to stay when leaving feels easier, or the choice to speak when silence feels safer.

In the next chapter, I'll share what it means to hold that pause, to live through the aftermath, and to face the shadows that try to follow us even after the storm has passed. Because healing doesn't stop with surviving—it deepens when we dare to voice it.

BLOOMING FORWARD

You don't owe anyone a polished version of your pain. Some chapters of your story aren't meant to be wrapped in silver linings or reshaped into neat, inspiring takeaways. They're meant to be honored for what they cost—for what they revealed—and for the strength it took to keep breathing through them.

If you've ever survived a season no one else knew about, if you've ever made it through a night that tried to take you under, you already understand: resilience doesn't always arrive as a grand victory. Sometimes, it's the simple, sacred act of waking up again.

There's power in staying. In showing up for one more morning, one more moment, one more quiet attempt to believe that your life still matters. And it does. Whether or not anyone clapped for you, the fact that you are still here is evidence that there is more for you—more joy, more softness, more spaces where you can finally exhale.

We often mistake survival for a delay in healing, but sometimes survival is proof that healing has already begun—before the words come, before the understanding takes shape. Sometimes, the bravest thing you can do is stay—with your breath, your body, your life. God sees that.

Psalm 73:26 (NIV) reminds us, *"My flesh and my heart may fail, but God is the strength of my heart and my portion forever."* You were never meant to carry everything alone. Needing help doesn't make you weak; it makes you human. And it means you're healing.

Author Glennon Doyle once wrote, "Being human is not hard because you're doing it wrong. It's hard because you're doing it right." Let that truth settle into your spirit. You've already done something remarkable—you stayed. Through the darkness, through the ache, even when no one noticed. That matters.

So, this week, offer yourself the kindness you've long withheld. Don't rush your recovery or minimize the milestones you've already reached. Don't wait until you feel "whole" to honor the distance you've traveled. Be proud of your endurance now. Your worth isn't earned through relentless strength—it's already yours, right here, as you are.

Take a moment to acknowledge the version of you who made it through. Speak to her with gentleness. Remind her: you didn't fail. You endured. You did what you could with what you had. You don't have to disappear to be good. You don't have to hide to be loved. The fact that you're still here doesn't mark the end of a chapter—it's the beginning of one written with more truth, one day at a time.

CHAPTER 6
Hope in Relationships

Relationships have always been one of the most beautiful and complicated parts of my story. I've experienced a connection so deep it felt divine, and I've also carried heartbreak so heavy it nearly made me forget who I was. Somewhere between those extremes, I learned this: hope in relationships isn't about perfection—it's about possibility. The possibility that even after betrayal, silence, distance, and disappointment, love can still find you. And this time, it can feel like peace.

As Darius Lovehall says in *Love Jones*, "When people who've been together a long time say that the romance is gone, what they're really saying is they've exhausted the possibility." That line has stayed with me because possibility is what hope breathes back into connection. Even when everything feels strained or empty, hope dares to imagine that love can still be rekindled—not perfectly, but honestly.

Getting to a place of healing required unlearning, layer by layer. There were years I didn't know what healthy love looked like. I knew performance. I knew the anxiety of wondering if I was "too much" or "not enough."

Being hurt by people who claimed to love you can cause even the most secure among us to question everything. You start to think love is something you have to earn—that safety is conditional, that being seen means being vulnerable, and vulnerability has always meant danger. I had to learn that real love doesn't require me to shrink. Real love doesn't keep me guessing. Real love doesn't ask me to abandon myself just to be chosen. Before I could believe in that kind of love from others, I had to begin practicing it with myself.

I had to stop romanticizing struggle, stop mistaking "chemistry" for chaos, and stop reaching for people who only wanted access to parts of me, not the whole woman I was becoming. That was hard, because sometimes we mistake familiarity for compatibility. We may gravitate toward people who mirror our wounds, not because they're good for us, but because they feel known. This is true for both platonic and romantic relationships. But just because someone feels familiar doesn't mean they're your future.

I've been loved in ways that almost broke me—not because the love wasn't real, but because it was wounded. People loved me through their own trauma, through their inability to see me beyond what they wanted me to be. For a long time, I tried to make that enough. I thought if I just loved harder, I'd be loved the way I needed. But love without safety is survival, and I was tired of surviving in spaces where love felt like a gamble.

There came a point when I had to admit the truth: love is not supposed to cost your peace. It's not supposed to silence your voice or stretch your spirit until it breaks. It's not supposed to make you question your worth every time you ask for more. I had to grieve the relationships that didn't survive my healing—the ones that made sense in my trauma but couldn't hold space for my truth, the ones I held onto out of loyalty even when they no longer fulfilled me.

Grieving that wasn't easy. Nobody talks about how painful it is to lose people who once felt like home. But I've learned that sometimes peace feels like distance. Sometimes growth looks like walking away. And sometimes hope in relationships means saying, "This is no longer enough for me." That acknowledgment is its own kind of freedom.

And then there were the ones who stayed—the friend who listened as if my unspoken moments were a language, the mentor who saw my gifts long before I had the courage to use them, the people who didn't flinch when I shared the ugliest parts of my story. They showed me that love can be gentle, that it can come without pressure, that it can say, "I see all of you—and I'm still here." That's when I began to believe again, not in perfect relationships, but in the possibility of them.

I began to understand that boundaries aren't walls; they're bridges to safety. They're love notes to your future self. And the more I honored mine, the more I attracted people who did too—the ones who didn't try to mold me into their comfort zone, who respected the shape of my healing even when it made them examine their own, and those who could sit with my truth without making it about their discomfort.

When you choose relationships not from longing but from discernment, everything changes. You stop chasing the people who drain your spirit and start nurturing the ones who fill your soul.

As I grew clearer about what peace felt like, I also grew clearer about what love should look like. In this season, I know what I need and will no longer apologize for it. I desire a man's man—one who leads with integrity, emotional intelligence, and compassion. Leadership doesn't mean control; it means guidance rooted in love. I want a partner who is protective yet peaceful, strong yet gentle, confident enough to stand beside me, not over me. A man who respects and cherishes Black women, who understands that to be followed, you must first be worthy of trust.

I'm drawn to strength that listens, to confidence that doesn't need to compete, to a presence that feels safe and steady. I want a man who values commitment, who understands that love is service and partnership, not performance. Someone who sees my ambition not as a threat but as an invitation to build something greater together. I admire a man with a strong work ethic, a grounded faith, and the courage to both lead and be led. Submission, to me, is not surrender—it's mutual trust. I want a love where both can lead with grace, where both can rest without fear, and where tenderness is never mistaken for weakness.

This kind of love doesn't rush or demand; it roots itself in peace. It honors the woman I've become while still leaving space for who I am becoming. That's the hope I carry now—not a love that tests my worth, but one that reflects it.

Knowing what I desire has brought new peace to how I love. It's no longer about striving or settling, but about honoring what feels true, reciprocal, and aligned with my spirit.

For me, faith became the foundation that steadied my relationships—not just faith in God, but faith in what love could be when it's rooted in something deeper than desire. Faith reminded me, even in conflict, to stay kind. It asked me to pause and reflect: *What does love require of me right now?* Faith sat with someone in their storm and said, *I won't leave.* It became the thread that stitched us back together when things fell apart, held space for forgiveness when apologies weren't perfect, and offered grace even when I was weary. Faith turned my relationships into more than exchanges; it turned them into meaningful ground for growth.

Part of that strength came from learning to set boundaries without guilt. For so long, I thought that saying no meant shutting people out. But I've learned that boundaries are bridges to honesty. They help people understand how to love you, while reminding you that your needs are valid. Boundaries reinforce your commitment to honoring yourself, even when it's uncomfortable. Saying no became an act of truth. My yeses became more intentional. I began trusting that I didn't have to sacrifice my peace just to be close to someone.

What I now understand is that hope is what allows relationships to grow. Hope believes we are capable of better, and it shows up in hard conversations. It walks with us through discomfort and doesn't require perfection—only presence. Hope says, *I believe in who we're becoming.* When you nurture your connections with that kind of hope, you're not just building love; you're building freedom. You're creating space where everyone can breathe, grow, and rise.

Hope strengthens relationships by helping us trust again. It softens fear without numbing wisdom. It rebuilds broken bonds, not by erasing what happened, but by honoring what can still be. With hope, we let go of survival patterns, release what no longer fits, and choose love that honors truth.

As you close this chapter on hope and healing, pause and take in how far you've come. You've redefined love on your terms—one that honors peace, mutual respect, and truth. You've learned to protect your heart without hardening it, to trust again without losing discernment, and to believe that connection can be both safe and sacred.

But every healed heart eventually meets a new invitation: courage. The courage to walk in your truth even when others misunderstand it. The courage to hold your standards steady when loneliness tries to whisper otherwise. The courage to stand firm in the in-between—the space between what was and what's yet to be.

That's where we're headed next. Because the hope that rebuilt your heart will soon meet the courage that carries it forward

BLOOMING FORWARD

Relationships shape us—sometimes through joy, sometimes through loss. Every experience, even the painful ones, leaves behind wisdom we can carry forward. The hope we hold for love is not a denial of what we've endured; it's a declaration that we still believe connection can be sacred, whole, and true. You don't have to rewrite the past to reclaim your future. You simply have to believe that love, in its healthiest form, is still possible—not perfect, but peaceful.

As bell hooks reminds us, "Love is an action, never simply a feeling." Sometimes, the first action is turning inward—choosing to love yourself with the same tenderness you once reserved for others. *Psalm 147:3 (NIV)* tells us, "He heals the brokenhearted and binds up their wounds." That kind of healing isn't about erasing what happened, but about remembering who you are beneath what hurt you. It's learning that real love won't ask you to dim your light, dilute your strength, or abandon your peace to be accepted.

Maybe you've known connections that stretched you beyond comfort—places where you gave too much, stayed too long, or lost sight of yourself in the process. And yet, something within you endured. That part of you—the one that still believes in connection that uplifts, protects, and respects—is not naïve. It's wise. It's hopeful. It's you, reborn through discernment.

Hope in relationships doesn't mean overlooking red flags or pretending disappointment didn't cut deep. It means moving forward with eyes open and a heart guided by wisdom. It's understanding that peace is your baseline, not your reward. Healing no longer feels like starting over; it feels like starting aligned. You no longer chase understanding—you attract reciprocity.

Ask yourself: *Does this connection honor my peace? Does it allow me to exhale? Does it reflect the same love I'm willing to give?*

Start where you are. Write yourself a promise: *I will no longer dim my light for the sake of being chosen.* Let go of performing for proximity. Say no without guilt, yes with intention, and allow people to show you whether they can meet you where you've grown. Let grace stay in the room, but let boundaries hold the door.

When you surround yourself with those who see you clearly and love you wholly, notice how peace becomes your rhythm. Notice how your faith deepens—in prayer, in your standards, and in the kind of love that doesn't compete with purpose but complements it. That is hope in motion, healing in bloom, and love restored to its rightful place.

PART TWO: COURAGE

"I realized that I don't have to be perfect. All I have to do is show up and enjoy the messy, imperfect, and beautiful journey of my life."
— *Kerry Washington*

CHAPTER 7
Courage in the In-Between

Thanksgiving and Christmas have always been my favorite time of year. The lights, the smell of good food, the sound of music and laughter—it all felt like a promise that love was still possible. I loved how families came together to share meals, offer thanks, and hold space for one another, even if just for a night. Those moments made me believe that joy could always return, no matter how much life had changed. But I also learned that not everyone saw the holidays that way. For some, Christmas wasn't about celebrating—it was about comparing. And without anyone saying it aloud, you could be made to feel as if love and belonging had to be earned.

I'll never forget one Christmas in foster care. I stood watching as presents were passed around—big, beautiful boxes wrapped in shiny paper and ribbons. The foster mother's grandchildren and the family's favorite foster child were called first, their arms full of gifts. Then came my turn: two small boxes, each barely bigger than a sheet of notebook paper. A shirt in one, maybe a pair of pants or another shirt in the other. And then came the comment that stung sharper than the cold outside: "Maybe if you were better, you would've gotten more."

Even as a child, I understood what that meant. "Better" didn't mean kinder or more deserving. It meant obedient. Compliant. Willing to clean up after the adults and play the part of the grateful orphan. But I refused. I would not shrink into their idea of what a foster child should be, nor let anyone mold me into a character they could manage. I was too proud, too sure of my own worth, for some adults to handle.

I stood there blank-faced, holding my little boxes as the room waited for my reaction. To excuse the other child's pile of gifts, someone added, "Her social worker got all that for her." As if that explained the inequity or justified the way they tried to make me feel small. For a moment, my throat tightened, words lodged somewhere between my chest and my mouth. I could feel every set of eyes in that room—some pitying, others smug—as if my reaction would determine whether they had won whatever game they were playing. I didn't give them the satisfaction. Inside, though, the sting settled deep, the kind that makes you wonder if you'll ever be seen as enough.

Even then, a seed of clarity took root: my worth wasn't defined by the size of a gift or the approval of adults who could not see my dignity. I didn't smile or cry. I simply stood there, knowing deep inside that love and care should never have to be earned.

That day taught me something I didn't yet have words for: you can't make people love you harder by being more perfect. You can't earn genuine care by performing or pleasing. The people who truly see your heart don't keep score. They don't measure you by how much you give, how well you perform, or how easy you are to manage. Christmas should have been about love, and love—real love—is given freely or not at all.

Now, when Christmas comes around, I decorate my home with intention. Every candle I light, every ornament I place, every small ritual I honor is for that little girl who stood there holding two small boxes. And I've carried that lesson into my work. For years, with the support of caring adults, I hosted Christmas events for children in foster care. In social services, I made sure every child on my caseload had their wish list fulfilled—not because gifts heal trauma, but because no child should feel forgotten or measured by how well they perform for love. I made sure they felt seen, valued, and celebrated. That's what I needed then. And that's what I can give now.

Not all my memories from foster care were centered around holidays. Some came from ordinary moments. Two boys used to ride their bikes past the house yelling "welfare child" and throwing rocks at me. I didn't know them; we'd never spoken. Yet their cruelty was consistent, like a routine. It went on for weeks, maybe months. One day, I was across the street visiting a friend when those same boys rode by, doing what they always did. But this time, I wasn't alone. Other kids were with me. One of them asked, "Who are they talking to?" I explained what had been happening.

That's when I learned the boys lived in a foster home down the street. They were in the same system, carrying the same label. So why were they attacking me? Before I could make sense of it, the confrontation escalated. Someone in the group shouted, "I bet you won't say that to our faces!" The boys got off their bikes, sticks in hand. They weren't looking for a group fight—they were still targeting me.

I've never been a tomboy, always soft in spirit even in hard places. But when they came at me, I fought. Not out of desire, but necessity. I fought with everything in me. I don't know if I got both, but I know I got one. After that day, they never bothered me again. A male neighbor stepped in at some point, but by then, I had already stood my ground. My hands ached, my chest pounded, but beneath the adrenaline was a steady knowing: I had defended myself. For the first time in a long while, I felt something shift—not toward fear, but toward strength.

Later, I moved to a new foster home. On my first day, the foster mother's son pitted me against another child already living there. He said, "I bet you can't beat her." I was confused. Beat her at what? Apparently, we were supposed to fight. It was like some twisted initiation. We tangled briefly—no one was seriously hurt—but her pride was bruised. From that day forward, I side-eyed everything in that house. That home wasn't all bad, but it was riddled with manipulation.

That night, lying in my new bed, I stared at the ceiling, my stomach tight. If this was the welcome, what else was waiting for me here? I had learned to read the undercurrents in a house. Survival depended on staying alert, never letting my guard down. They played foster kids against each other, expected us to clean up after adults, and withheld nice things from those who didn't obey. But I refused to be treated like an Orphan Annie story. I was a child, not a servant.

Then came deeper betrayals—the kinds no child should have to navigate. One weekend, the other foster girl asked me to go with her to babysit at one of the foster mother's adult daughters' homes. Both daughters' husbands were there when we arrived. They said the kids were out with their mom and we could just relax until they returned. But something felt off. As soon as we entered, the men left, laughing. We walked into the entertainment room to find the TV playing porn. I was disgusted. When I asked the other girl about it, she shrugged. "They do that all the time," she said.

I was furious. What kind of grown men did that to children? I wasn't even a teenager yet, just a child trying to make sense of what no child should see. It was grooming, predatory behavior. They never touched me, but the message was clear: we were being tested, watched, devalued. From that moment, I was vigilant around those men. I moved through the rest of the weekend with heaviness in my chest. No one asked why, and I wouldn't have told them if they had. That's the thing about certain betrayals—you carry them as unspoken truths that shape how you move through every room afterward.

Some memories still sit raw in my chest, like the time the son of a trusted neighbor tried to force himself on me. I fought him and got away, but the betrayal lingered. I felt as though I had been set up. The scent of him—his body, his sweat—stayed with me for years, heavy and sour, a sensory reminder I never asked to keep. Even now, if I see a photo of him or cross paths with his family, that memory returns in an instant. It reminds me how the body never truly forgets what the heart has had to survive. He is a father now, and sometimes I wonder—if he has a daughter, how would he respond if she told him that a man had done to her what he once tried to do to me? Would he recognize the weight of what he caused, or the strength it took for me to fight back? The thought stays with me, not out of bitterness, but because I believe accountability is part of healing too. Even as I retell it now, I know I did nothing wrong. I spoke the only way I could: through resistance.

Despite betrayal, manipulation, loneliness, and self-doubt, I kept showing up. That's the courage I want to speak to next: the kind that faces fear head-on. Healing doesn't mean the fear disappears; it means you no longer let it control the story. In the next chapter, we'll step into that space where courage meets vulnerability—and where possibility is born.

BLOOMING FORWARD

Courage often grows quietly, not in the roar of victory but in the resolve to keep standing when the world tries to knock you down. It shows itself in the decision to protect your own spirit when others dismiss, overlook, or try to make you feel "less than." You were never the smallness they projected onto you. You were already a gift—and you still are.

That is the kind of strength that doesn't seek applause. It rises when no one is watching. In a world that often treats children—especially young girls—as disposable, you became a woman who refused to disappear. You have endured moments that could have hardened you, yet you chose tenderness. You met betrayal where there should have been protection and still made space for joy. Not the kind you must perform for others, but a grounded joy that honors memory and defies shame. A joy that beats like a steady rhythm beneath your days, an act of resilience all its own.

And here is the truth: your survival restored not only you, it also prepared you to walk beside others in their healing. The season that once made you feel invisible became the foundation from which you now help others feel seen. As Audre Lorde reminds us, "Caring for myself is not self-indulgence, it is self-preservation, and that is an act of political warfare." Sometimes that care begins with naming what hurts without apology. Healing is not about forgetting but about reclaiming the narrative. The shame was never yours to carry—it belongs to those who failed to protect you.

Psalm 30:11 (NIV) says, "You turned my wailing into dancing; you removed my sackcloth and clothed me with joy." Joy, in this light, is not denial but defiance—a reclaiming of what was once stolen. When you revisit the little girl holding two small boxes and tell her, *You were always the gift*, you are transforming pain into power without erasing the memory.

If no one has told you: you did not deserve what happened. You were not the cause of the cruelty or the manipulation. You survived—and that survival is not the ending but the beginning of something richer. From here, you decide who has access to your peace, who earns a place near your joy, and who walks beside your healing. Boundaries are not bitterness; they are clarity, care, and self-respect.

So today, make space for a joy that coexists with your memories and still shines. Celebrate that you are no longer merely surviving—you are becoming. Becoming someone who can sit with her truth without shrinking. Who can tell her story and still sing, knowing that joy is not granted by others; it is your birthright.

Choose one small ritual that feels like reclaiming joy on your terms. It might be preparing a meal you love, decorating your space in a way that reflects your spirit, or saying no where you once felt obligated to say yes. Let it remind you: you no longer seek approval. You are honoring your worth, choosing joy that belongs wholly to you.

CHAPTER 8
Embracing Courage

I once believed courage looked like boldness—standing on stages, speaking without hesitation, doing the hard thing with ease and a smile. Over time, I learned courage does not always arrive in big, visible ways. It looks like getting out of bed when every part of you wants to hide beneath the covers. It is saying no when yes would keep the peace, or sitting with yourself long enough to admit what your heart truly desires.

Courage is not the absence of fear; it is the decision to move forward beside it. There were seasons of my life when I let fear lead—not in every area, but in the ones that mattered most. I was not afraid of being judged for who I was—I have always walked to the beat of my own drum—but I did worry about being counted out because of where I came from. I didn't want my journey through foster care, abuse, or pain to become the reason someone saw me as less than. So I played it safe and colored inside the lines. I didn't step as fully or as boldly as I could have. I tempered my light and called it wisdom—told myself I was being responsible, humble, cautious—but in truth, I was protecting parts of my story that others might not understand. I knew how to stand tall, yet I had not allowed myself to expand without apology.

Choosing courage meant allowing myself to be seen in every part of who I was: polished and raw, healing and strong. The whole me. A woman with stories and scars, with tenderness and truth, with dreams once buried and boundaries just beginning to form. The first time I created a real boundary with someone I loved, I cried—not because they reacted badly, but because I had never chosen myself that way before.

It felt like both a loss and a gain—shedding a version of me that had kept me safe for years but no longer served me. That is the thing about courage: sometimes it asks you to release who you were taught to be so you can become who you truly are. Courage made me uncomfortable, but it also made me free.

One of the most courageous things I ever did was start telling the truth—the kind that makes your voice shake, rearranges relationships, and finally sets you free. I remember the first time I told someone about what I had endured, the pain I had carried behind my smile. My hands trembled. I did not know if I would be believed or if they would see me differently. But I spoke anyway. Silence had begun to suffocate me, and when I finally released my truth, something shifted within me. I had made space for myself and reclaimed the part of me that had carried the weight alone. That is what courage does—it gives your truth room to breathe.

But courage does not appear only in dramatic moments. It lives in the quiet decisions: leaving a relationship that no longer honors you, refusing to apologize for being too emotional or too passionate, allowing yourself to say, "I want more," without shame.

For many years, I thought boundaries were nothing more than walls—cold, rigid, unyielding. But I learned boundaries can be tender too. They do not have to be sharp to be strong. A boundary says, "I love you, but I will not abandon myself to keep you close." Courage taught me that.

It also taught me how to walk away—not from anger, but from misalignment. Not because I did not care, but because I finally did. The more I embraced courage, the more I had to grieve: grief for the people who only loved the version of me who asked for nothing, grief for the comfort of familiarity even when it was rooted in pain, grief for the silence that once felt safe but slowly stole my voice.

On the other side of that grief came clarity, peace, and the rediscovery of myself. Courage is not always a battle cry. Often it shows up in small, consistent choices—starting something new without all the answers, admitting a mistake and learning from it, standing firm in your values when others disagree. These moments may not carry the drama of a spotlight, yet they are profound in their own way. Every step taken in truth, no matter how small, is a step toward freedom.

What does everyday bravery look like for you? It might be making the phone call you have avoided, speaking up in a meeting, or choosing rest even when the world insists you keep going. Each time you show up for yourself, you are practicing courage.

Let's be honest: vulnerability is frightening. Opening up, sharing fears, admitting you do not have it all together—it all feels risky. Yet vulnerability is one of the most courageous things you can do. It is how trust is built, how relationships deepen, and how growth begins. Vulnerability opens the door to transformation. When we lower our guard, even slightly, we create space for healing and connection. We invite others into the most authentic parts of who we are.

Courage and vulnerability are inseparable. You cannot have one without the other. It takes bravery to let someone see you—not just the curated version, but the tender, unpolished parts. And that is where the light gets in. That is where freedom begins.

Faith became my steady anchor when courage felt out of reach. When I was unsure of the next step and fear tried to grip me, I leaned into what I believed. I turned to scriptures that reminded me I was not alone—like Joshua 1:9: "Be strong and courageous. Do not be afraid; do not be discouraged, for the Lord your God will be with you wherever you go." I breathed those words in. I repeated affirmations: *I have the strength to face what lies ahead. I trust the process.* In those moments of stillness, I could feel my spirit renewing.

Faith does not erase uncertainty, but it gives you something solid to stand on when the ground beneath you feels unsteady. It speaks to your soul: *You are held, guided, and never alone.* Sometimes that assurance is enough to keep going.

Remember to celebrate the wins—the boundaries you honored, the truths you spoke, the times you chose yourself instead of settling for less. These are not small things; they are acts of personal revolution. Courage deserves to be recognized. Write it down. Say it aloud. Dance in your living room if you want to. Let each moment of bravery become a marker of how far you have come.

Even when doubt or fear creeps in with its old lies, you have a trail of truth to look back on. You have done hard things before, and you can do them again. Living stuck in fear was never your purpose. You were made to live boldly, rise repeatedly, and choose courage one breath at a time.

You have honored the bravery that lives within you—the courage that speaks through truth, boundaries, and the quiet strength to walk away from what no longer honors your becoming. Courage is not about never feeling afraid; it is about showing up anyway, with a steady heart and faith that you were made for more than surviving.

Still, even when courage leads, self-doubt sometimes follows. It questions your worth, whispering, *Who do you think you are?* In the next chapter, we will face those inner critics and rewrite the scripts that once kept us small—because you are not your fear; you are the one who rises anyway.

BLOOMING FORWARD

"Courage is not the absence of fear, but the triumph over it," wrote Nelson Mandela.

Courage often arrives quietly, in moments no one else will ever witness. It is telling the truth you once avoided, honoring a boundary that costs comfort, or choosing rest when the world insists you keep pushing. These are not grand gestures meant to impress; they are private revolutions that transform life from the inside out.

Think of a recent moment when your voice was unsteady, yet you spoke anyway—when fear urged you to retreat, but you stayed present. That trembling was not weakness; it was evidence of your bravery. The sound of you refusing to disappear from your own life.

Look back on those moments not with criticism, but with reverence. When was the last time you chose yourself in the face of discomfort? Let that memory become your anchor. Every act of honesty is a reclamation of self, and sometimes the greatest courage is found in refusing to abandon who you are to keep others comfortable.

Boundaries are part of that courage. They are not cold walls meant to keep people out, but invitations to deeper respect. Saying, *This is where I end and you begin,* is one of the clearest ways to affirm your worth. Whether the boundary takes the form of silence in chaos, declining to over-explain, or stepping away from what no longer serves you, remember this: setting a boundary is not selfishness—it is wholeness that requires clarity. Sometimes it means grieving relationships that were only whole when you asked for nothing. That grief is real, but it makes space for something greater—peace, alignment, and the freedom to show up fully alive.

As Joshua 1:9 (NIV) reminds us, "Be strong and courageous. Do not be afraid; do not be discouraged, for the Lord your God will be with you wherever you go."

Courage is not something you must wait for; it is something you can practice, one day at a time. You do not have to feel ready or fearless—you only need to take one honest step toward the truth. That step might be applying for something new, letting go of something old, or allowing yourself to rest without guilt. You are allowed to move gently on your journey.

Do not let fear convince you to stay still. You were not made for stagnation but for becoming. Let today be the day you try—one action is all it takes to start. That is how courage grows, and that is how you bloom: boldly, beautifully, and without needing permission.

CHAPTER 9

Facing Fears and Self-Doubt

Fear once sat in the front row of my life. It had an opinion about everything—my dreams, my choices, my voice—and more times than I care to admit, I listened. Though I believed in myself, fear still found its way into my reasoning, shaping how I protected and presented myself.

Fear rarely arrives looking like a monster. More often, it sounds like wisdom: *Play it safe. That's too much. Be realistic.* Sometimes it dresses up as self-doubt: *You're not ready. Someone else can do it better. Don't embarrass yourself.* We call it caution or humility, but it is fear in disguise—wearing clothes that feel familiar.

Self-doubt offers no warning. It's like the imaginary angel on one shoulder and critic on the other, questioning your voice even as you write. Before you speak, it urges you to edit your truth. It waits until you're right on the edge of blooming and then whispers a *what if.* I've felt it—right before saying yes to something I'd prayed for, before sharing a piece of my story that still makes me pause, before claiming space I had earned.

Fear would tap me on the shoulder and replay every failure, every moment of being overlooked or left behind. It attacks your actions and your perception of self. But here is what I have learned: just because fear speaks does not mean it's telling the truth.

Fear holds us back, yet understanding its roots is the first step to releasing its grip. It often grows from past experiences—moments of embarrassment, rejection, or disappointment. Sometimes it's fed by outside voices insisting we must look, act, or achieve a certain way. We all carry versions of it: the fear of failure—*What if I mess up and everyone notices?* The fear of rejection—worrying that putting yourself out there means being ignored or turned away. The fear of uncertainty—stepping into something new without knowing how it will end.

When I began facing my fear, I stopped letting it run the show. I started asking, *Is this fear—or a lie I've rehearsed so often it feels true?* That question changed everything. I learned to move forward even when doubt was still in the room. I began responding to fear with faith, not because I was unafraid, but because I believed something greater waited on the other side. Faith doesn't erase fear—it reminds you that you are larger than it.

I'll never forget the day I had the opportunity to say yes to something big—something I had prayed for and wanted deeply. Yet I froze. All I could hear was that familiar voice: *You're not ready. You don't have the credentials. They'll find out you're not as together as you seem.* That voice didn't just speak—it moved through hesitation, procrastination, and perfectionism. It lived in the way I second-guessed every decision and every word.

Then something shifted. I paused and asked myself, *What if it goes right?* Not in a naïve way, but in a grounded, Spirit-led way. What if I stopped assuming the worst and trusted that I already carried what I needed? What if I stopped disqualifying myself from rooms where I had been divinely placed? So I said yes. My knees trembled, my voice shook—but I said yes anyway. Fear may raise its voice, but I choose who holds the mic.

Fear is rooted in memory—it reminds you of what was, not what's possible. Faith is rooted in vision, pulling you forward and planting seeds where fear insists nothing can grow. You don't conquer fear by pretending it doesn't exist; you overcome it by naming it, facing it, and moving anyway. Each step you take with fear in the background reminds you who is truly in control. Self-doubt may visit, but it does not get to stay, and it certainly doesn't get to write your story.

We all have that inner critic—the voice determined to highlight every flaw and magnify every fear: *You're not good enough. You'll mess up again. Why bother trying?* The critic thrives on repetition and keeps us stuck. But within us also lives an inner ally—the voice of reason, compassion, and truth. It says, *You've got this. You're learning. You've overcome before—you'll do it again.*

Fear wears many faces. Sometimes it's triggered by people close to us; other times it rises from the unknown. But fear loses power when you stop hiding from it. When you name it, understand it, and move in spite of it, you strip it of the control it once had. You replace its weight with truth, strength, and grace.

Many of us grew up surrounded by fear-based language: *Don't get your hopes up. That's just the way things are. Be careful how much you dream.* We internalized those cautions and built lives around staying small. But what if you gave yourself permission to want more—without fear as your filter? What if you stopped assuming every blessing carries a catch? What if you believed joy, peace, and purpose were available to you not because you are perfect, but because you are present?

I have seen how faith quiets self-doubt and replaces it with trust—not only in yourself, but in the journey itself. It reminds you that you are not alone as you face challenges, and that even in uncertainty, there is a plan unfolding. Faith doesn't mean you are fearless; it means you keep walking, even when your knees feel unsteady. Each time you show up, speak up, or take a leap, you honor not just your strength, but your calling.

So take the step. Write the truth. Speak the dream. Apply anyway. Share anyway. Begin anyway. You have already survived what fear told you was impossible—now it's time to thrive.

Fear thrives in silence, but you are not silent anymore. You have named the lies it told you and replaced them with truth. You've learned to speak back to doubt and to move forward in faith, even in uncertainty. That is no small thing—that is transformation. You are no longer bracing for impact; you are learning to hope again.

Let your actions declare: *I am no longer ruled by fear.* Even if doubt lingers, your movement says otherwise. You are growing. You are rising. And you are no longer living as if fear is the narrator of your story. It does not hold the pen—you do.

In the next chapter, we'll explore how choosing action—especially imperfect, brave action—becomes more than a moment. It becomes a rhythm. Because courage isn't a destination; it's a way of living. And your next step? It's already waiting.

BLOOMING FORWARD

Fear doesn't need volume to have power—it only needs repetition. The more we rehearse its messages, the more they sound like wisdom. Often, we don't realize we've given it a seat at the table until hesitation, second-guessing, or shrinking appears. But you don't need to be fearless to move forward; you simply need to be honest—honest about what you feel, about the roots of that fear, and about the moment you decide, *I don't want to live like this anymore.* That honesty is not weakness; it is strength. Once you name fear, you strip it of its mystery, and once you see it clearly, you can choose differently.

Overcoming fear is rarely one grand decision. More often, it's a collection of small, steady choices that build strength over time. Each moment you show up for yourself, you develop a new muscle: resilience. As Eleanor Roosevelt said, "You gain strength, courage, and confidence by every experience in which you truly stop to look fear in the face." That kind of strength doesn't come from perfection but from choosing to try again after fear has told you not to.

Maybe you've been asking, *What if I fail?* But what if that's the wrong question? What if instead you asked, *What if I fly?* Fear prepares you for the worst, but faith opens the door to possibility. That shift is the invitation—to lean into hope and believe that something beautiful is still possible. It's not naïve to expect goodness; it's brave and necessary.

Fear convinces us that we must be perfect before we begin, yet progress lives in the messy middle—one small act of courage at a time. One decision to write the page, speak the truth, or say yes even when you're unsure. Scripture reminds us in 1 John 4:18 (NIV), "There is no fear in love. But perfect love drives out fear." Not through force, but through presence. When you root yourself in love—real, unshakable, God-centered love—fear loses its footing.

Let this be the season you choose presence over perfection. You don't need all the answers, and you don't have to silence every doubt. You need one brave step forward. Hit send. Speak up. Sign up. Trust the nudge stirring in your spirit. You've already survived what fear said you couldn't—now it's time to thrive.

Let your actions declare: *I am no longer ruled by fear.* Even if doubt lingers, your movement says otherwise. "You are growing. You are *evolving.* And fear is no longer the narrator of your story. It doesn't hold the pen—you do.

CHAPTER 10

Taking the First Step

I remember a time when I talked myself in circles about something I wanted to do. I prayed and journaled about it, even asked for signs—and they came. Yet still I hesitated. What unsettled me wasn't the risk of failing but the possibility of becoming. Stepping into that version of myself meant letting go of every identity I had built around playing it safe. I kept waiting for perfect conditions, for the fear to vanish, for confidence to arrive first. But confidence doesn't precede the step; it grows because of it.

When I finally moved, I discovered something I had forgotten: I am stronger in motion than I ever am in hiding. That beginning step didn't fix everything or erase doubt, but it offered evidence that I could keep going without waiting for approval, perfection, or applause. Sometimes the first step is the prayer itself—an exhale, a break in the pattern. The step is meaningful because it signals a shift, a refusal to stay stuck, a choice to believe in more even while the *more* is still unfolding. Taking the first step isn't about proving anything; it's about remembering who you are and acting like it's true. No one else may notice—but you do. Heaven does. And that is enough.

What I didn't realize back then was how many invisible chains I had wrapped around myself—beliefs passed down, disappointments internalized, stories never challenged. Before I moved forward, I carried them as if they were truths. I believed that if something didn't come easily, maybe it wasn't meant for me. If I didn't know the *how*, then I must not be worthy of the *what*. Yet some things only make sense after obedience. Some blessings only appear once you begin to move.

I used to pause on the edge, heart pounding against my ribs. The voice of fear told me to wait, but somewhere beneath it, a quieter knowing urged me forward. I wasn't made to live in a cage of safety. I wasn't made to keep surviving without fully living. The moment I listened to truth over noise didn't erase uncertainty, but it loosened its hold.

Not everything fell neatly into place after that first step. But I stopped waiting to feel ready and started walking in alignment with what I knew, even when my footing felt uncertain. I learned to trust the process more than perfection and to celebrate steps as much as outcomes. In that space, I found a freedom I hadn't known I craved—the freedom that comes from releasing the version of yourself that stayed small just to feel safe.

There is something profound about deciding fear will not have the last word. Something transformative about standing before what once paralyzed you and saying, "I'm still going." Your voice may tremble, your knees may shake, and even if the staircase is hidden in shadow, that move remains the beginning of becoming—not someone new, but someone more whole. More you.

The greatest surprise wasn't the step itself but what it unlocked within me. Facing what I feared reshaped my inner landscape. It didn't only build courage; it cleared away the lies I had believed about perfection, certainty, and needing others stamp of approval on my every move. As that clutter lifted, I realized fear wasn't truth—it was habit.

That realization changed how I moved forward. I stopped waiting for dramatic breakthroughs and began honoring motion, however small. Each time I honored my yes, my no, or made space for my truth instead of shrinking, I became braver, softer, and more honest about what I wanted. That momentum created something steady inside me. And even when fear returned—and it still does—I had proof I could keep going.

Standing at the edge of a dream feels both thrilling and terrifying. The first step carries the weight of your hopes and the shadow of your doubts. You imagine all the ways it could go wrong, all the people who might not understand, and all the fears disguised as logic. But most of that fear is smoke and mirrors. Once you step through it, you see how little power it truly held.

We make beginnings bigger than they need to be. We picture a giant leap when often what's required is one deliberate act. That's the beauty of micro-movements—you don't have to do it all at once or see the full map ahead. You only need the next right step: open the document, make the call, speak one brave truth aloud. The size doesn't matter; the shift does.

Faith, I've learned, is the bridge between hesitation and motion. It says, "Start here." Faith doesn't guarantee ease; it promises presence. You may not know the ending, but faith doesn't require certainty to begin—only willingness. Think of every bold soul who ever changed the world. They didn't have all the answers, but they had conviction, a reason larger than fear. They knew the initial step mattered.

Now I celebrate every single step forward. It doesn't have to be glamorous or complete. Start a "Small Wins" list and record each moment that proves you are moving: "Sent the email." "Made the call." "Showed up for myself." These may look simple, yet they form the foundation. The more you honor your progress, the more you trust yourself when fear tries to talk you out of becoming.

And I want you to have that same proof—not from perfection or highlight-reel moments, but from the quiet voice within that says, "I think I'm ready." Or even better: "I'm not ready, but I'm willing." You don't have to have it all figured out to begin. You simply have to believe that movement itself is holy and that the life waiting on the other side of your forward motion will honor the one brave enough to take it.

Even the smallest action can spark transformation. Beginning is often the hardest part, but it's also the most rewarding. That first meaningful step may feel uncertain, but it matters because it means you're no longer standing still. Once you begin, you invite momentum, growth, and grace into motion.

Challenges will come, but so will clarity and faith. In the next chapter, we'll explore what it means to stand strong through life's storms—not because you are perfect, but because you are anchored in purpose.

BLOOMING FORWARD

Taking the initial move may not silence every doubt, but it awakens something far more powerful: evidence—proof that you are capable of growth, still in motion, still becoming. It doesn't have to be graceful or certain. What matters is that you moved, trusting your spirit's nudge more than fear's voice. You decided your future deserved more than your retreat. We often imagine boldness as thunderous declarations or cinematic gestures, yet sometimes it looks like breathing deep, opening the door, and saying yes to the next right thing.

You don't have to see the end of the path to take the next step along it. Anchor yourself in this truth: your life is worthy of movement. Nothing is too small when it comes to beginning again. A journal entry counts. Speaking your truth counts. Refusing to explain away your dreams counts. These micro-decisions may seem ordinary, but they build an extraordinary rhythm of resilience. They teach your heart it is safe to try again. And that trust you're building in yourself—that's the one thing fear cannot survive in.

I once thought I needed permission, validation from others, or a sign written in bold print. But the truest invitation came from within, a quiet clarity that urged, *Go.* That voice didn't appear because I was fully prepared; it came because I was still enough to hear what was calling me forward. When I moved, the fog didn't vanish instantly, but the ground beneath me steadied—as if it had been waiting for my first step.

Anne Lamott once wrote, "Almost everything will work again if you unplug it for a few minutes... including you." That truth stays with me. Sometimes we must disconnect from the versions of ourselves that only know how to hustle or survive, and reconnect with the one that longs to live. She's still here, listening for your yes.

Scripture reminds us in Isaiah 30:21 (NIV), "Whether you turn to the right or to the left, your ears will hear a voice behind you, saying, 'This is the way; walk in it.'" That voice invites participation. You are not required to have all the answers—only to respond. Walking in purpose isn't about the absence of fear; it's about the presence of faith that steadies you as you grow.

So today, reflect on your almost moments—the conversations you nearly began, the opportunities you almost pursued, the dreams you could have claimed. Choose one and ask yourself: *What small, deliberate move can I make toward it this week?* Not a leap, but a steady step that says, "I'm listening. I'm willing." And when you take that step, however ordinary it feels, remember—the life you're reaching for is already reaching back.

CHAPTER 11

Standing Strong Through Storms

S trength is not what I once believed it to be. I used to think it meant silence—holding it all together, getting up even when I hadn't rested, smiling while my heart was breaking, showing up for everyone else even when I had nothing left to give. That was the version of strength I had mastered; the kind built on survival, not sustainability.

But survival has an expiration date. Eventually, it wears on your body, your spirit, your joy. At first, you may not notice. You keep pushing, performing, pretending. Yet over time, the cracks begin to show. I reached that point—the moment when the storm wasn't just raging outside of me, but swelling inside. All the disappointments I had swallowed, betrayals I had minimized, pressure I had normalized—everything I had shoved down for the sake of being "strong" surged back with force. And in the stillness, when the noise around me faded, a question I had been afraid to ask rose up: *What happens when the strong one breaks?*

Because I was breaking.

Not in ways most people could see. I was still showing up, still smiling, still checking every box. But inside, something was unraveling. I laughed less. My prayers grew shorter, less expectant. I stopped dreaming. My body was present, but my spirit felt far away. I wasn't standing strong; I was standing still. And I had confused the two.

Storms have a way of stripping everything down—not to destroy you, but to reveal what's real. What I learned in one of my hardest seasons is this: real strength doesn't come from how much you can hold, but from knowing when to release. It's not about pushing through in silence, but about letting yourself be held. It's telling the truth and resting without guilt. Saying, *I'm not okay right now,* and allowing someone to meet you there. It's the courage to unclench your jaw, exhale, and admit the load has become too heavy.

What saved me was the slow peeling away, one layer at a time. I stopped asking how I could carry more and started asking what I could finally set down. I stopped glorifying struggle and began opening my hands to receive. And perhaps most importantly, I stopped viewing storms as punishments. Sometimes they aren't punishments at all, but clarifying interruptions—a clearing before the blooming.

There were days when breathing felt like an act of faith. The storm had settled into my chest. My back ached from the invisible weight I'd carried for years. My shoulders stayed tense, bracing for the next blow. I was living in a body trying to survive a life that no longer fit. Despite that, I kept going until the day came when pretending was no longer sustainable.

I had to unlearn what I thought strength was. It wasn't about appearing unaffected. It wasn't about denying my emotions or pretending to be the one who always had it together. I was hurting, grieving, and angry. And the bravest thing I did was admit it and let the tears come. I embraced the stillness and allowed myself to fall apart. I surrendered. And when the wave of pain passed, what I felt wasn't weakness—it was relief; the deep relief of no longer having to hold it all alone.

Breakdowns used to mean failure to me. Now I understand they can be tender pauses; your soul's invitation to stop carrying what you were never meant to hold. In reality, a breakdown isn't the end at all—it can be the last honest pause before a breakthrough. It's that moment when everything in you says, *Let's stop pretending. Let's stop pushing. Let's stop calling this survival joy.* And when you allow yourself to honor that pause, a new way of being starts to unfold.

The storm didn't destroy me. It revealed me, stripping away every illusion I'd built about strength and showing me something quieter, softer, more enduring. Strength is not in the armor—it's in the return to truth.

I rebuilt, brick by brick, with boundaries in place. I stopped explaining myself to people who only admired my strength but had no care for my tenderness. The applause from those who didn't know my cost no longer mattered. I listened to my body again and made space to meditate, to hear His words, and heed His signs. I chose to rise slowly, ask for help, prioritize joy—even when it felt too small to matter. I chose softness when the world insisted I harden, because that's strength, too.

Just as my internal storm exposed what I was carrying, I saw how life's tempests test every vessel that dares to stay afloat. At times, life is like a ship crossing open waters. You expect the waves, but then the sky darkens and the winds shift. The storm comes, floods the deck, tears the sails, and makes you feel like you're going under. But when the storm passes, the winds hush, the waves settle—and you're still afloat. Maybe battered, worn, but still moving forward.

That's resilience.

And like that ship, I learned to trust my anchor: my faith to hold. When grief and uncertainty threatened to pull me under, I stopped asking to be rescued and began praying for clarity and courage. In that fragile season, I found solace in words that met me exactly where I was: *"My grace is sufficient for you, for my power is made perfect in weakness."* (2 Corinthians 12:9 NIV). That promise steadied me like a lighthouse in the dark.

Faith didn't end the storm, but it gave me something to hold onto when nothing else made sense.

Turning points seldom announce themselves. Mine arrived in the driver's seat of my car, after a conversation that uncovered a truth I could no longer ignore. My hands gripped the steering wheel, torn between wanting to revisit the conversation and knowing silence would be my own undoing. The tears that followed weren't for an individual or situation—they were for the version of me who kept choosing to carry what needed to be released. The air felt heavy, my pulse steadying as truth finally caught up to me. In that moment, I realized the people I wanted most beside me couldn't go where my healing required me to go. The weight of that truth pressed in. I could either collapse into silence or choose to rise.

And yet, the choice wasn't simple. Rising meant letting go of what was familiar, even if it no longer fit. It meant grieving the picture of togetherness I had held onto for so long. Silence, on the other hand, promised temporary peace—but at the cost of myself. Sitting there, the tension between the two pulled at me—loyalty to others on one side, loyalty to my own soul on the other.

The pull was piercing, but clarity came with it. I could not keep betraying myself for the comfort of others. To rise meant to honor the woman God created and was calling me to protect, even if it cost me closeness with those unwilling to walk beside me. Now I knew the way forward would begin with truth.

And the truth is this: storms don't just test us—they transform us. They eliminate what is no longer needed, free us from roles we were never meant to carry, and invite us to live authentically instead of performing. They reveal what we've outgrown, what we've carried too long, and what we no longer need to prove. You've stood your ground in the winds of life. But now, another kind of healing calls.

This is where the journey shifts—not in proving, not in pushing, but in the strength to let go. Strength that bows out of survival and learns to rest without guilt. Strength that opens the cracks wide enough for light to seep through, reminding us we are not machines; we are human, cherished, and worthy of tenderness.

BLOOMING FORWARD

Strength isn't always what we've been taught. It's not only loud declarations or unshakable presence—it's often the quiet decision to set something down. The moment you admit the weight is too much and you choose to rest instead of perform. If you've been holding it all together for too long, it's okay to stop striving and simply be. Rest isn't weakness. Rest is what makes healing possible.

For many of us, no one modeled what it looks like to let someone else share the weight. But strength isn't about never bending—it's knowing when to step out of survival mode and into something softer, something real.

I once believed that if I ever let myself cry, everything would collapse. But when the tears came, the opposite happened: life began, piece by piece, to come together.

Storms don't always destroy what matters most. More often, they strip away what never truly did. And in that clearing, space opens for something new to take root. I think back to the day I sat in my car, realizing I could no longer shoulder everyone else's expectations while denying my own exhaustion. There was no applause, no sudden clarity—only a pause that steadied me. I knew I wasn't alone. God was with me.

Leonard Cohen once wrote, *"There is a crack in everything. That's how the light gets in."* In those words is an invitation: to stop hiding the cracks and start honoring the light they let through. We don't have to fix everything before we can feel whole. We only have to be honest. Honesty is its own kind of healing—it lets the light in, opens our hearts to receive, and reminds us we are not machines. We are souls. Souls that grow softer, stronger, and more rooted when we choose truth over performance. That kind of strength changes everything.

Those words echoed after countless sleepless nights; they weren't just a verse—they were a rescue. Scripture tells us in *Matthew 11:28 (NIV)*, *"Come to me, all you who are weary and burdened, and I will give you rest."* Not a lecture or another assignment, but rest. That's what awaits on the other side of release.

If you've been pretending everything is okay when it isn't, this is your invitation to exhale. To be human. To stop explaining and simply exist. You don't have to hold it all to be worthy. You are allowed to need care and to not be okay. And in that honest space, God meets you with open arms.

This week, pause with intention. Turn down the noise. Sit with yourself and ask one question: *What am I tired of carrying alone?* Let that be your starting point. You don't need to fix everything. You just need to tell the truth. That's how strength returns—bit by bit, one exhale at a time—until even the storm feels like the clearing before new growth.

And that's when you realize strength was never about holding tight—it was about trusting the hands that hold you, even as you learn to release and begin again.

CHAPTER 12
Finding Freedom in Letting Go

There's something no one tells you about release: it can be as meaningful as the holding—but only when you're ready to tell the truth about what the holding has cost you.

I held on to so much for so long. Old expectations. Silent roles I never volunteered for. Friendships that became one-sided—people who stayed close as long as my light benefited them, but drifted when they realized it wouldn't make them shine. I didn't hold on out of fear of being left with nothing; solitude has never frightened me. I held on because I cared, because I believed in who they could be, even when the truth told me it was time to let go.

But enduring isn't always the assignment. Survival can teach us to stay too long, work too hard, and carry what was never ours. Only when we pause and reflect on the journey do we hear the truth beneath the noise. And that truth says: you don't have to carry this anymore.

There's a freedom that comes when you stop over-explaining yourself and stop shrinking to fit someone else's comfort. You stop measuring your worth by how much you can hold. And let me tell you—that kind of freedom doesn't come with a celebration or a parade. It shows up quietly—with peace, the knowing that you don't have to perform healing anymore. You simply get to be.

Letting go doesn't mean you stop caring; it means you stop bleeding for things that don't bleed back. It means you stop watering what's been draining you and stop writing chapters in someone else's story so you can start living your own.

Here's the beautiful part: when you finally release what was, your hands—your heart—are open for what can be: the right people, the right path, and the version of you that isn't tied to suffering.

You start to feel lighter, not all at once like a weight vanishing overnight, but little by little: breathing easier, sleeping without heaviness, smiling in ways that feel more true. Because you've stopped hiding and started living in alignment—the most powerful freedom there is.

I didn't learn to let go all at once. It came in layers. A silence that followed arguments. The ache of conversations where my words never landed. The fatigue of showing up for everyone but myself. Each time I dismissed my own needs to keep the peace, I was learning. Each time I stayed in places that drained me, I was learning. Letting go was never a single act—it was the slow, steady recognition that peace should not come at the expense of my wholeness.

There's also the buy-in process—the tug-of-war between what you know in your spirit and what you're still trying to convince your heart to accept. You tell yourself maybe things will change, maybe this time will be different, maybe the weight isn't really that heavy. It's the cycle of bargaining we all know too well. We call it patience or loyalty, but often it's fear disguised as hope. And yet, even in the back-and-forth, you're learning. Every hesitation, every second-guessing thought is part of the unraveling that leads you closer to release.

Peace should never come at the price of your soul. Yet many of us—especially women—were conditioned to be agreeable, to maintain peace at any cost, to hold families and communities together even while unraveling inside. Generations taught us to confuse sacrifice with strength, and we called it love and loyalty. But often, it was fear in a pretty dress.

I knew this not just in theory but in my own life. There's this one day I'll never forget. I was standing in my kitchen, on the edge of tears after a lengthy conversation that left me empty again. I was trying so hard to explain myself, to be understood, to make it work. And I just ... stopped mid-sentence. Something in me shut all the way down—not from anger, but from the realization: they would never hear me, and I no longer needed them to. That realization felt like freedom. When you stop seeking validation from those who misunderstand you, you reclaim your power. You stop rehearsing speeches they'll never receive. You stop softening your truth to fit someone else's fear. You start walking in clarity, understanding that not everyone is meant to go with you.

The truth of the matter is, sometimes we outgrow what the relationship was built on.

Letting go doesn't have to be complicated. At times, it's silence—a phone call you don't return. Behavior you no longer entertain. A seat at the table you politely push away from, not out of resentment, but because you realize you deserve better than crumbs. And it's not just people we release; we must let go of who we thought we had to be. The strong fixer holding it all together. That identity might've helped you survive, but it's not who you are.

You are allowed to grow beyond what you needed to be in your hardest season.

Letting go is not about becoming someone else. It's about becoming more fully you. If you're standing at that edge right now, unsure if you should loosen your grip on something or someone, let this be your invitation: you don't have to wait until it breaks you. You can choose peace before it gets that far.

Freedom isn't only found in leaving. It can be found in releasing the weight that no longer belongs to you. What's left isn't loss—it's room. Room for discovery, peace, and an opportunity to step into the life that calls you forward. A life of fulfillment.

Because here's what I've learned: emotional burdens don't always look like chaos. Sometimes they look like constantly second-guessing yourself, over-apologizing, staying quiet when you want to speak, or smiling when you feel like screaming. They show up as grudges, regret, and guilt. And these things live in our bodies. At first, they're small, almost unnoticeable. But over time, they grow heavy, weighing us down and slowly reshaping how we show up—not just for others, but for ourselves.

Holding onto pain is like carrying a stone in your pocket. You think it's manageable. But step after step, day after day, it gets heavier. And when you reach in and set it down, you realize how much lighter life can feel.

And sometimes, the hardest person to forgive is you.

We replay our mistakes, magnify our failures, and talk to ourselves with a harshness we'd never use with anyone else. We say things like *I should've known better. Why did I let that happen? I'm too much. I'm not enough.* And we think accountability means self-punishment.

But freedom lives in self-compassion—not excuses or denial, but kindness. And here comes grace. Grace reminds us that we are human beings who are learning, evolving, and worthy of love—even in the midst of our mess.

What if you started speaking to yourself with gentleness? If you replaced "I messed up again" with "I'm learning"? Whispered "I forgive you," not to them, but to yourself?

Forgiveness doesn't mean forgetting. It means choosing to no longer be held hostage by what hurt you. It means saying, *I may not be able to change the past, but I can decide how I carry it.*

And it's not all-or-nothing. Radical acceptance—that's where it begins. Just a deep, honest release of the fight to control what cannot be changed. That's when you begin to heal. And in that return, you make room—not only for what's next, but for who you're becoming.

Letting go isn't the end of the story; it's the beginning of your return—a return to alignment, to peace, to grace. When we release what no longer serves us, we don't just create distance from the past; we make space for what was always meant to stay.

BLOOMING FORWARD

There comes a moment when you realize you've been holding on, not because it's still right, but because it's familiar. Roles you never asked for, silence worn like a second skin; the belief that your worth was proven by how much you could endure. And even when that weight begins to ache, release isn't always immediate. We cling to what we've always known. Letting go can feel less like freedom at first and more like grief—like standing at the edge of everything you thought you had to be and wondering who you are without it. But you're not losing yourself. You're releasing what was never yours to keep.

So, take a steady breath. If your hands have been wrapped around old expectations, outdated roles, or relationships that demand your silence to survive, let me encourage you to loosen your grip. Release doesn't have to be boisterous or final. Bell Hooks once said, "Sometimes letting go is an act of far greater power than defending or hanging on." That kind of power is subtle, often unnoticed, but deeply transformative.

God meets us in these tender returns. Not with pressure, but with promise: "... let us throw off everything that hinders and the sin that so easily entangles. And let us run with perseverance the race marked out for us" (Hebrews 12:1, NIV). This is freedom in motion—shedding what was never yours to carry so you can step into what has been waiting all along.

If you find yourself standing between what you've always carried and what your heart longs for, choose yourself. Choose rest and alignment without explanations or proving. Begin where you are. The version of you untethered from exhaustion is already waiting.

As Part Two closes, may you carry courage forward—not as armor, but as trust in your own unfolding.

PART THREE: GRACE

"Love is like the sea. It's a moving thing, but still and
all, it takes its shape from the shore it meets, and it's
different with every shore.".
— Zora Neale Hurston

CHAPTER 13

Grace in Every Season

G race found me in the places I didn't think I deserved it. Not in the polished chapters of success or the neatly packaged versions of myself I tried to present to the world. It found me in the mess—in the unraveling, in the seasons I was raw and uncertain, aching and unsure. And instead of judgment, I felt held.

I once believed grace was something to earn. I thought I had to pray the right way, show up the right way, or fix myself before I could rest or feel worthy of love. But grace doesn't wait for perfection. It meets you in your pain and reminds you that your heart is still worthy, even now.

For years, I struggled to extend that same grace to myself. I replayed mistakes like a worn-out song, holding guilt as if it proved responsibility and measuring worth by how much I carried and how little I asked for in return. That cycle drained me until something gave way—a soft reckoning. I needed more than survival. Grace stepped in quietly, like light pouring through blinds on a morning I thought I couldn't get out of bed. Like a friend saying, "It's okay to be tired. You don't have to explain." Like breath reminding me I was still here. Grace isn't a reward; it's a return—to spirit, softness, and humanity.

When I began accepting grace—from God, from others, and slowly from myself—I started to understand what it means to be human. Not perfect, but whole. Messy, beautiful, and still becoming.

Have you been holding yourself to standards no one else can meet? Have you made your worth conditional on healing faster, doing more, or hurting less? What would it look like to loosen your grip and say, *Even as I am... I deserve grace*? You don't have to prove anything to be worthy of rest, nor explain your wounds to deserve healing. You don't have to carry it all. Grace is the permission slip that says, *Just be.*

Grace doesn't erase pain; it helps you carry it differently. I used to think healing meant I'd always feel light and free—that I'd never be triggered, tired, or thrown off course again. I thought if I just "did the work," I'd graduate from the parts of me that still hurt. But healing is not a straight line; it moves like waves. And grace is the shoreline that welcomes you every time you return.

Even now, doubt sometimes creeps in. Old questions rise: *Am I doing enough? Have I healed enough?* In those moments, grace wraps around me and whispers, *You are not a project; you are a person.* That truth changes one's perspective.

Grace taught me I don't have to be "on" all the time. I can show up undone and still be loved. I can rest without guilt. Tears don't mean I've gone backward—they mean I'm still healing. Healing doesn't move backward; it moves in rhythm. And grace moves with it.

Some days, grace looks like canceling plans. Other days, it's saying yes to joy you didn't think you deserved. Sometimes it shows up in therapy, or in laughter returning after a long silence. However it arrives, grace never asks you to be fixed. It asks you to be honest—to feel, to trust, and to let it be messy and yours.

I think of every version of myself—the girl who stayed silent, the woman who kept pushing, the soul who almost gave up—and I want to gather them all close and whisper: *You didn't fail. You survived so you could breathe life into your becoming.* That, beloved, is grace.

For too long, I measured worth by how much I could endure. Smiling through heartbreak. Holding everything together when I was falling apart inside. I thought endurance was proof of strength. But grace offered another way: strength that doesn't demand silence and worth that isn't tied to performance.

Grace met me in the in-between and reminded me that healing isn't about constant breakthroughs or breakdowns—it's about honoring the middle ground, the space where growth takes root before it shows. The in-between is where you're no longer who you were but not yet who you're becoming. It's where uncertainty lingers and faith whispers louder than certainty. Grace met me there—not to rush me forward or pull me back, but to remind me that even the waiting is holy, even the ordinary days are part of transformation.

Grace is never afraid of your process; it honors it. At its core, grace is unconditional love—forgiveness you don't have to earn, healing that finds you in your most human moments. It is the rain that softens hardened ground, bringing refreshment and renewal you didn't know you needed. Grace doesn't demand perfection; it simply asks you to receive.

Like the prodigal daughter, stumbling home with regret and empty hands, we are met by a Love that runs toward us with open arms—no lectures, no shame, only joy that we came home. That is grace: not earned, but freely given. Sometimes the hardest part isn't receiving grace from others or even from God—it's learning to receive it from ourselves.

Truthfully, self-forgiveness may be one of the most radical forms of mercy we'll ever practice. It means releasing the lie that you are only lovable when flawless. It means choosing compassion over criticism. It means saying, *Yes, I made a mistake... and I still deserve peace.* Try this: write yourself a letter. Say the words you wish someone had said in your lowest moment. Let grace flow through your own voice. Let healing begin with you—and then carry that same grace into the world.

Grace doesn't just comfort—it calls. It reminds you, *You are not your worst day.* It lifts your chin and whispers that transformation is still possible.

Once you've tasted grace, you'll find yourself pouring it out—in kindness, in forgiveness, in gentleness toward yourself and others. You'll notice that pausing before reacting feels natural, compassion softens how you listen, and the voice you use with yourself grows kinder. That's the quiet work of grace, the slow becoming of peace.

Even when we know grace, it can still be hard to accept it after we fall. But that's where it shines brightest. It's the unearned gift of love and forgiveness—the hand that lifts, the presence that steadies, the light that keeps us soft.

Take a moment to acknowledge how far you've come—from the silent tears to the mornings you rise despite the weight. Grace in every season means every version of you has been seen, held, and invited to heal.

In the next chapter, we'll explore what happens when we stumble even after grace—and how those moments become the soil where rebirth begins.

BLOOMING FORWARD

There are moments when you're convinced you don't deserve a second chance—yet grace arrives anyway. Not with applause or grand gestures, but in ways that shift everything. Maybe it was a kindness offered when you felt unworthy, or the first deep breath after carrying guilt too long. That, too, is grace. It doesn't demand flawlessness before showing up; it meets you where you are, offering rest without condition.

What's most surprising is how ordinary it feels in the moment—it simply begins to lift the weight you thought you'd always carry.

Anne Lamott once wrote, *"I do not understand the mystery of grace—only that it meets us where we are and does not leave us where it found us."* That is its beauty: grace doesn't wait for us to clean the mess before entering the room. It doesn't pull back when it sees our shame or fear. It steps closer, speaking to the parts of us we thought too broken to be touched. In its presence, the edges inside begin to soften.

Scripture promises, *"Let us then approach God's throne of grace with confidence, so that we may receive mercy and find grace to help us in our time of need"* (Hebrews 4:16, NIV). You don't have to earn the right to enter that space; you simply come.

And when you do, you discover grace isn't rationed—it flows without hesitation or limit.

Our culture often measures strength by endurance—by how much you can carry or how well you can hide your pain. Grace offers another way. It invites you to set the burden down, even for a moment, and breathe again. It reminds you that tears aren't weakness; they're release. That naming your hurt isn't self-pity; it's honesty. That tending to your heart isn't indulgence; it's stewardship.

Grace lives in the affirmations you whisper to yourself: *I am allowed to heal. I am allowed to be seen. I am allowed to rest.*

The most transformative grace is the kind you extend inward—not once, but over and over. It doesn't need to be grand to be real. Grace can look like choosing a slower pace when everything in you wants to rush. It can sound like "no" without explanation or feel like writing the dream you've been afraid to name. Sometimes it's as simple as sitting still and remembering that you are loved.

Grace isn't earned through achievement; it's received through surrender. And when you let it stay, it rewrites how you see yourself—not as someone hustling for worth, but as someone who already carries it.

That is grace. Let it find you. Let it remain.

CHAPTER 14

Grace in Failure

There was a time when disappointment cut me deeply. I didn't believe failure defined me, but I still took every closed door to heart. If something didn't work out—a job, a relationship, an opportunity—I carried it openly because I've never been one to hide my feelings. I often wondered if the outcome might have been different if I had pushed harder or given more of myself. I wore those disappointments like evidence that I could have done more.

Over time, I realized how often we *qualify* our failures. We explain them away, try to make sense of them before the sting has settled, as if wrapping our pain in reason will make it easier to hold. We tell ourselves, *"Maybe I wasn't ready," "Maybe it wasn't meant for me,"* because the truth—that something we loved or worked for fell apart—feels too raw to face. But grace doesn't need your justifications. It meets you in the unfiltered ache and invites you to rest there long enough to see what's real.

Grace taught me to pause before claiming fault. It asked me a question that changed everything: *"What if this isn't failure—what if this is redirection?"* The first time I heard those words in my spirit, I cried. Not because they erased the pain, but because they offered another way to see it—not as punishment, not as proof I was broken, but as part of becoming. It was an unfolding, not a falling apart. In that moment, I realized grace wasn't reserved for the polished and perfect. It was a lifeline for the weary—an invitation to see my stumbles as ground for growth.

Looking back, I can see how each closed door carried mercy disguised as loss. The love I tried to force, the "yes" I gave when I should have said "no," the dream that unraveled—all of them made space for alignment I couldn't yet imagine. What once felt like ruin became reformation.

Failure didn't ruin me. It revealed me. It showed where I was still hustling for approval, where my worth was tied to performance, and where fear still held the mic. And grace—she didn't rush me to fix it. She stayed with me in the quiet, offering the patience I refused to give myself. No grand comebacks, no quick lessons, just presence. What I needed wasn't resolution. It was gentleness.

There's something steady about learning to stay with yourself in the aftermath of disappointment. Not running. Not numbing. Not pretending. Simply sitting with the ache and remembering: you are not your outcome. You are someone still learning, still growing, still worthy. That's what grace does—it holds you when self-criticism tries to take the lead.

You don't have to turn every loss into something beautiful right away. Grace doesn't demand performance; it reminds you, *"Even here, you are loved."* It means it—even when plans change, even when the door closes and you're left unsure of what comes next. Especially then. That is when grace draws closest. That is when she wraps herself around your exhaustion and says: *You're still whole. Still chosen. Still becoming.*

The hardest part of failure isn't the fall—it's what we tell ourselves afterward. I didn't just sit in disappointment; I built a house in it. I replayed every misstep, feeding myself the cruelest words: *"You should've known better. No wonder things fall apart."* I would never speak that way to someone I love, yet I spoke it to myself without hesitation. Those words became walls that kept me small. I thought I had to earn grace through perfection, to show up flawless if I wanted to be loved. But grace never asked for that. She came for the undone, aching, neglected parts of me—and she stayed.

I remember one failure in particular, the kind that left me exposed. It wasn't just the disappointment that hurt—it was the shame. The sting of having dared to hope, to believe, to try, only to watch it unravel in front of others. I had prayed over it, spoken life into it, shared it with faith—and when it still fell apart, I felt like I fell with it. Public failure, private grief.

But in the stillness that followed, something shifted. I stopped trying to package the pain into a lesson. I didn't have the strength to be inspirational. I let the grief be heavy, raw, unpolished. And that's where grace met me—not with answers, but with presence. She didn't hand me clichés or tidy resolutions. She simply stayed near and reminded me, *"You don't have to fix this to be worthy of peace."* That was enough.

Not every ending is poetic. Not every loss needs to be redeemed right away. Sometimes, surviving it *is* the miracle. Choosing to try again tomorrow, even when your voice trembles, is strength in motion. Healing doesn't always announce itself—it arrives quietly, like light filtering into a dim room, revealing what's left and what's still possible.

Eventually, you catch yourself laughing again. You breathe deeper, and it no longer feels like a battle. You glance in the mirror and see someone softer, wiser, still standing. That is grace—steady, unhurried, and faithful.

Maybe failure didn't come to destroy you. Maybe it came to reveal the places where you've been shrinking to fit, saying yes when your soul was pleading for no. Maybe failure wasn't the enemy—it was the flashlight showing what needed healing. Maybe it exposed the parts of you that were choosing fear and calling it faith. Perhaps it was never punishment at all. Perhaps it was preparation.

Redefining failure became one of the most liberating spiritual shifts of my life. For so long, I carried the word like a scarlet letter—shame, guilt, embarrassment stitched to it. But now, I see failure as fertile soil. It's not the end of the story; it's the ground where resilience takes root.

The women I admire most—those who've changed culture and carved space for others—have stories lined with rejection and redirection. Oprah Winfrey was told she wasn't fit for television. Ava DuVernay didn't direct her first feature film until her thirties. Viola Davis faced years of invisibility before her talent was recognized. And Tina Turner, after years of silence and survival, rebuilt her career on her own terms. None of them were untouched by failure. But grace taught them to stay in the story—to keep creating, keep believing, and keep showing up until the door that was meant for them opened.

Grace invites us to reframe what didn't go as planned. What looked like loss might have been protection. What felt like an ending might have been a doorway. What seemed like a fall might be clearing space for you to rise differently. Setbacks don't cancel your calling; they refine it. Scripture reminds us, "I can do all things through Christ who strengthens me"

(Philippians 4:13). Not just the visible victories, but the quiet comebacks, the trembling rebuilds, the faithful try-agains.

Faith doesn't promise an easy path. It promises presence—strength for this step, not just the destination. You are not disqualified by your detours. You are deepened by them.

The next time you stumble, try saying this: *"I am growing. Each misstep is preparing me for what's next."* Because grace isn't a quick fix. It's the steady bridge that carries you forward.

The hardest forgiveness is often the one you owe yourself. We replay our mistakes, stack guilt upon regret, and believe that punishment is the only proof of accountability. But grace invites you to lay that burden down—not because the pain didn't matter, but because *you do.*

Self-compassion in the face of failure doesn't excuse what happened; it transforms how you hold it. It asks, *"What did this teach me?"* instead of, *"Why can't I ever get it right?"* Healing starts with honesty, not perfection. Speak to yourself as though grace has already begun its work—because it has. The breath in your lungs and the resilience in your spirit are evidence of it.

Failure isn't final—it's formative. That door that closed might have been protection. That "no" might have been a divine pause clearing space for your "yes." Grace rarely shouts its arrival; it settles in as a deep knowing: *You're not being rejected—you're being redirected.*

Grace says: You don't have to be finished to be worthy. You don't have to be flawless to be held. Take a breath, not to fix, but to reflect. Think of a season that changed you. Maybe it stripped away illusions you didn't need. Maybe it unearthed strength you didn't know you carried. Whatever it revealed, honor it. Let that truth remind you: failure isn't your undoing—it's your refining.

This journey isn't about making pain pretty. It's about recognizing the transformation that took root in hard soil. It's about naming the growth that bloomed where you thought nothing could survive. With that truth in your hands, step forward—not defined by perfection, but anchored in grace. You are not broken. You are becoming.

Even after the fall, there is grace. When paired with failure, it becomes a teacher, not a verdict. It reveals what you've outgrown and where deeper healing calls. The detour isn't your disqualification—it's your development.

In the next chapter, we'll explore what comes after the fall: the pause. Because after failure, we don't rush—we rest. We let stillness do its quiet work. Before the next rising, there is a season of surrender, and that, too, is grace.

BLOOMING FORWARD

Failure can feel final, but grace teaches us it's often just an inflection point—the moment you stop hustling to prove your worth and start remembering you already have it. The most freeing shift comes when you stop trying to *qualify* your pain—when you no longer need to justify the detour to validate the lesson. What looks like loss may be protection. What feels like delay may be divine alignment.

We've been taught to measure success by outcomes—the job gained, the goal met, the dream fulfilled. But grace values meaning over metrics. It honors growth over applause. When life takes a turn you didn't plan, grace reminds you, *"Pause here.*

Something sacred is happening beneath the surface." You are not behind. You are becoming.

Jack Kornfield wrote, "To live life is to make a succession of errors. Understanding this can bring us great ease and forgiveness for ourselves and others." Grace carries that same truth: you are not a mistake because something failed. You are a miracle because you keep beginning.

If you're holding disappointment, give it a name. Write it down, pray it out, or simply speak it aloud. Then, beside it, write what it taught you—what strength surfaced, what faith grew. When you're ready, say, *"I release this. I honor what it gave me. I choose grace."*

Scripture reminds us, "My grace is sufficient for you, for my power is made perfect in weakness" (2 Corinthians 12:9, NIV). Your story isn't over because something ended. Grace is still writing. You are still blooming—tender, wise, and wholly becoming.

CHAPTER 15
Learning to Rest and Reflect

R est was something I thought I had to earn after crossing everything off my list and being everything to everyone. It was a prize at the end of exhaustion—a permission slip for the overachiever in me who believed worth was tied to how much I could do. For years, I wore fatigue like an accomplishment. I believed if I just worked hard enough, long enough, and needed nothing from anyone, I would finally deserve peace. But the truth is... the exhale *is* the work. And rest? Rest is resistance. Rest is reclamation. It's remembering that you are not a machine—you are a miracle in motion.

It took me years to stop glorifying the hustle and treating depletion as proof of devotion. I once believed exhaustion meant progress, but I was really running from myself—from the grief I hadn't faced, the truth I hadn't spoken, the silence I feared might reveal what I wasn't ready to admit. Stillness unnerved me because I didn't know what would rise to the surface once the noise faded. But stillness, I've learned, is not an enemy. It's a mirror. When the noise quiets—the outside expectations, the inner criticism, the pretending—you begin to hear your own heartbeat again. You remember who you are beneath the roles. Rest isn't laziness; it's listening. It's checking in with your spirit, honoring your body, and returning to yourself.

There were seasons when slowing down felt dangerous, like everything I built might crumble if I dared to stop. But grace taught me that what's meant for you will not slip away just because you paused. Peace doesn't operate in panic. It moves at the pace of trust. There is something profoundly powerful about the woman who chooses rest on purpose—who no longer waits for burnout to justify it, who knows she doesn't need crisis to earn calm. I'm still ambitious, still building, still dreaming, but now I understand that legacy and stillness can hold hands. True success leaves room to breathe.

As we learn to rest, reflection becomes the natural rhythm that follows. Reflection is how the soul makes meaning—it's how we gather wisdom from what we've lived through. It asks gentle questions: *What did this season teach me? What do I need to release? What deserves to be remembered?* Reflection isn't always ritual; sometimes it arrives uninvited. It happens on a journal page, during a quiet drive, or when folding laundry in silence. It's not about control; it's about paying attention. And the more you do it, the more you see how far you've come—how many storms you've survived, how many times you've chosen grace over guilt and love over fear.

I once believed my value was tied to my productivity. That stillness was wasteful. That pausing meant failure. But grace kept tugging at me, reminding me that my worth was never connected to what I produced—it was rooted in who I was becoming. And becoming doesn't happen in a rush. It happens in the quiet—in the long exhale that feels like release and return at once. Rest doesn't erase your drive; it renews it. It reminds you that your spirit, not your schedule, deserves to lead.

Clarity often comes only when everything else stops moving. When you turn off the notifications and silence the inner critic, you make space to hear truth again: *You are tired. You are worthy. You are allowed to rest.* But arriving at that truth required honesty. Beneath the busyness lived unhealed pain—old wounds, buried grief, unspoken disappointment. I kept busy because I was afraid of what would meet me in the quiet. Yet stillness didn't break me—it revealed where I'd been holding myself together with threads of survival. It showed me the spaces where healing was waiting.

I remember one evening sitting in my car after work—engine off, eyes closed, too tired to move. I didn't need a plan. I didn't need to fix anything. I just needed to breathe. That single breath felt like defiance. Like saying, *"I don't have to prove anything right now. I just get to be."* And that was enough.

Rest taught me that nothing true is lost in the pause. The pause is where we reclaim what we once believed had to be sacrificed—our peace, our clarity, our connection to God. Because rest makes room for revelation. It's where divine wisdom finds open space to speak. Scripture reminds us, "Be still, and know that I am God" (Psalm 46:10, NIV). It doesn't say *do more* or *earn more*. It says *be still*. That's where presence meets peace.

There is sacredness in choosing rest, especially for women who have been told they must always endure, provide, and persevere. When you lay your head down early, cancel a plan without guilt, or sit in silence instead of striving, you are declaring: *I matter. My peace matters. My joy matters.* Rest is not weakness—it is prophetic. It says, "I trust that what's meant for me won't vanish if I pause."

Reflection is how we honor that trust. It's how we look back and say, *That version of me was doing her best.* It's where we tell the truth about what hurt and what healed. It lets us sit beside our former selves with tenderness instead of judgment. From that seat of grace, we can ask: *What is worth carrying forward? What do I need to set down?* Reflection is not indulgence; it is stewardship of the soul. It transforms memory into meaning.

You don't need a perfect process to begin. Sometimes reflection is journaling through tears. Sometimes it's sitting in silence with your thoughts. Sometimes it's the pause before sleep when you let your mind unclench. Rest is not a luxury; it's a necessity for renewal—mental, emotional, spiritual. It's what allows you to keep showing up whole.

Think of a tree in its dormant season. On the surface, it appears bare, but beneath the soil, its roots deepen, storing strength for what's to come. That's what rest does for us. It grounds us for the next bloom. When was the last time you rested without guilt—not just closed your eyes, but truly exhaled? Not just took a break, but allowed yourself to feel held?

We are not meant to earn rest; we are meant to live in rhythm with it. When we rest, reflection follows—through journaling, walks, prayer, or simply breathing and noticing. Reflection doesn't always bring answers, but it always restores alignment. Stillness isn't empty; it's full of potential. Faith grows strongest in the pauses where we stop striving and learn to trust the unseen. When we surrender to rest, we remember we are held—not by achievement, but by grace.

Rest isn't the absence of doing; it's the presence of awareness. When we pause long enough to listen, to breathe, and to notice what's stirring beneath the surface, we rediscover our own humanity. Rest clears the fog. It renews our sight. It reminds us that presence matters more than performance. And that might be the heart of it: learning that the pause is part of the work. Stillness isn't where life stops—it's where life begins to make sense again.

In the next chapter, we'll explore how gratitude deepens this perspective. Gratitude grows out of reflection—it's the fruit of slowing down long enough to notice what remains beautiful. Gratitude doesn't dismiss pain; it reveals grace within it. When rest and gratitude meet, something in us softens and begins to bloom again.

We can create intentional moments of rest: slow mornings with tea and quiet, tech-free evenings with music and candlelight, walks in nature that remind us we're part of something larger. Let rest be the soil where your peace takes root and reflection be your compass. Because healing doesn't live in the hustle—it lives in the pause. Rest doesn't just restore; it transforms how we see. It opens our eyes to wonder, gratitude, and the quiet joy of being alive.

BLOOMING FORWARD

There is something revolutionary about choosing to rest in a world that glorifies exhaustion. Not just physical rest, but soul-deep rest—the kind that says, *"I matter, even when I'm not producing."* Real rest isn't collapse after burnout; it's a conscious act of reverence before you reach the edge. It's no longer waiting for a breakdown to honor what your spirit has been asking for all along: time to breathe, time to feel, time to simply be.

The moments we slow down—curling up under a blanket with no agenda, letting the dishes wait, giving ourselves permission to pause—are where clarity finds us. In that stillness, your spirit begins to speak truths the noise had buried: *You are tired, but you are still whole. You are still good. You are still worthy of tenderness.* In that honesty, rest becomes not just care, but courage.

Poet Nayyirah Waheed wrote, *"And I said to my body, 'I want to be your friend.' It took a long breath and replied, 'I have been waiting my whole life for this.'"* That is what rest sounds like—the moment your body exhales and believes you.

You don't need a plan to rest; you need presence. Tell yourself the truth: you deserve rest, not because you've earned it, but because you are already enough. In that space, reflection begins to bloom. You start to notice what no longer fits, what burdens have expired, what dreams still carry light. Some of the goals you once chased were born from survival, not joy—and it's okay to release them. Reflection is how we honor what shaped us without carrying its weight forever.

This week, create one intentional pocket of rest. Sit outside and breathe deeply. Write a letter to the version of you who kept going when she was tired. Let your words become a prayer of gratitude for her endurance and a promise to rest more freely moving forward.

Exodus 33:14 (NIV) says, "My Presence will go with you, and I will give you rest." That rest isn't absence—it's a gift. It's the steady rhythm of grace reminding you that you're not alone. Take it. Treasure it. Trust that what waits on the other side of stillness isn't emptiness—it's renewal.

CHAPTER 16
Grace in Gratitude

There was a time when I thought gratitude meant pretending everything was fine—that it required me to ignore the ache, downplay the hurt, or spiritualize my way through suffering. *"Be grateful,"* they said, as if it were a bandage for wounds that hadn't even stopped bleeding. But grace taught me something different. Gratitude is not denial. It doesn't minimize what went wrong or dismiss how something broke your heart. Gratitude is the courage to find something worth holding onto anyway. It's the ability to look at your story—mess, miracle, and all—and say, *Even here... there is something good.*

But I've learned that gratitude begins in moments of solitude—in the smallest acknowledgment that even here, even now, there is something good.
For me, it often started in memory. The smell of sweet potato pie baking in my grandmother's kitchen. The way her prayers filled a room, thick with hope. Gratitude helped me remember that I came from people who knew how to make joy out of

what they had, who sang through scarcity, who believed in the power of one more try. Even when life felt uncertain, gratitude tethered me to that strength.

I remember the mentor who told me I had a gift long before I believed it myself. I remember laughing with friends when joy felt impossible. And I remember waking up—sometimes in tears—and realizing that even in the sorrow, I was still here. Still breathing. Still becoming.

It took time to reach that point. Because gratitude isn't only about giving thanks when life goes well; it's about honoring what remains after things fall apart. It's seeing the lesson hidden in the letdown, the truth tucked inside the disappointment. It's finding yourself in the aftermath and saying, *I'm thankful I made it.*

I don't always feel grateful in the moment. Some days, I have to reach for it. I sit with the discomfort and ask, *What is still true? What have I survived? What beauty is trying to show up, even now?* Over time I've learned that grace and gratitude walk hand in hand. Grace says, *You don't have to earn your worth.* And gratitude answers, *Thank you for loving me anyway.* One creates room for the other. When you live in that space—slowing down enough to notice what's holding you up—it changes how you see everything.

Suddenly, the ordinary becomes holy: a cup of coffee, a phone call, a night without chaos, a "yes" after so many "no's." Miracles don't always arrive wrapped in ribbons. Sometimes they come when you don't know how you're going to pay a bill or feed your family. When the test results say *no cancer.* When you're approved to buy a home—no down payment required. Or in something as simple as the first bloom of spring—the reminder that life renews itself even after long winters.

One morning, I stopped for breakfast at a drive-thru. I was exhausted and heavy with thoughts I hadn't said out loud. When I reached the window, the cashier smiled and said, "The car in front of you paid for your meal." It caught me off guard. I'd heard of people doing this before, but it had never happened to me. That small gesture—unexpected and unprompted—shifted my entire outlook. I felt seen, lifted. Two days later, I did the same for the person behind me. Gratitude is contagious like that. It has a way of multiplying joy simply because someone chose kindness.

And when life still hurts—and it will—gratitude becomes an anchor. A way to say, *This moment isn't everything... but it's something. And I'll honor it.*

Now, I make space for gratitude even when I'm grieving. I thank God for the clarity that came through conflict, for the boundaries I learned to draw, and for the version of me that rose from the ashes. I don't rush to find all the answers, but I do look for a ray of hope—the kind that says, *I've been kept. I've been covered. I've been carried.*

I don't need everything to be perfect to give thanks anymore. A grateful heart isn't one with less pain—it's one with more perspective. It sees the full picture and still finds beauty in the brushstrokes. Gratitude doesn't erase the struggle; it reminds you the struggle isn't the whole story.

Gratitude has also become a practice of presence. It invites us to slow down and notice what we might otherwise pass over. It reminds us we are not waiting for a perfect moment to feel blessed—we are already standing in one. Even now. Even here. There's a subtle kind of strength that rises when we give thanks in imperfect seasons. When we're still waiting for the healing, still holding our breath between breakthroughs. It's in those very places where grace steps in—not with answers, but with awareness. And suddenly you see how much you've grown, how far you've come, and how many times you thought, *This is the end... and it wasn't.*

At times, gratitude is bold—like laughter after loss, dancing in your living room for no reason, or testifying about the way God made a way out of no way. Other times it's gentle: a folded blanket at the edge of the bed, a phone call you didn't expect but needed, a full belly, a soft yes, a deep exhale. Stillness after months of noise. There was a season when all I could say was, *Thank you for carrying me.* I didn't have words for much more, but I didn't need to. Gratitude isn't about proving worth; it's about presence. It's not how eloquent your thanksgiving sounds; it's how true it feels when you speak it to yourself in the dark.

Gratitude also means honoring your own strength. You don't have to wait for someone else to validate your resilience or recognize your progress. You don't have to wait for a perfect outcome to be proud of your process. You don't need the struggle to be over before you say, *I've done something beautiful with what I've been given.* Grace lets you say thank you for this version of yourself—the one still healing, still hopeful, still here.

Beyond emotion, gratitude is a transformative practice with real impact on our well-being. Studies show that people who practice gratitude experience greater happiness, reduced stress, and even improved physical health. It shifts our focus from what's missing to what's present. In one study, participants who wrote down three things they were grateful for each day reported feeling more optimistic within weeks. Another found that gratitude lowered cortisol levels, easing anxiety and tension. Gratitude isn't just something you feel—it's something you live.

When was the last time you paused to appreciate the simple joys around you? Whether it's the warmth of sunlight on your face or the kindness of a stranger, gratitude has the power to brighten even the most ordinary day. And while it's easy to feel grateful when life is good, what about during seasons of hardship? Gratitude can feel distant when you're navigating loss or uncertainty. Yet it's in those very times that gratitude becomes a tool for finding hope and strength.

When we live with that awareness, something shifts. Grace and gratitude form a beautiful cycle. Grace teaches us to receive life's gifts with humility, while gratitude helps us recognize and cherish them. Together, they shift our perspective from scarcity to abundance. Think about the moments when someone extended grace to you—perhaps they forgave a mistake or offered kindness when you needed it most. How did that make you feel? Likely, it sparked gratitude that deepened your connection to them. This is the grace–gratitude cycle: grace fosters gratitude, and gratitude inspires us to extend grace to others.

As we begin to notice the small gifts around us—a smile, a meal shared, a moment of peace—it transforms how we see the world. Even ordinary days begin to feel extraordinary. Gratitude is most powerful when it's put into action. Feeling grateful is one thing—expressing it is another. By turning gratitude into practice, we not only enrich our own lives but also uplift those around us.

Maybe for you, it's writing a thank-you note. Maybe it's keeping a journal or simply telling someone you love them. These small offerings become part of the rhythm of a heart that remembers. Take a moment today to write down one thing you're grateful for and notice how that single step opens your heart.

Here's the beauty of it all: gratitude doesn't just transform your life—it creates a ripple that touches others. When you express gratitude, you uplift the people around you, inspiring them to do the same. Think about the last time someone thanked you—didn't it leave a lasting impression? Perhaps their words motivated you to continue offering kindness. Gratitude is contagious. A simple thank you or thoughtful gesture can brighten someone's day and encourage them to pass it on. By practicing gratitude, we contribute to a world that feels more compassionate, connected, and hopeful.

So much of healing begins with noticing—choosing to pause long enough to honor what is still good, still present, still worthy. Gratitude doesn't need a stage. It lives in the hush after the storm, the inhale before a new beginning. When we see life through that lens—not only what's missing, but what remains—we begin to move differently. Softer. Kinder. More whole.

That's the beauty of gratitude. It doesn't just change how we view our circumstances; it transforms how we show up in them. It softens our reactions, deepens our compassion, and expands our ability to extend grace to others. And as we first began to explore back in Chapter Eleven, grace has never been about perfection—it's about presence. It meets us where we are and invites us to do the same for others. Because once you've been carried by grace, it's hard not to offer it in return.

BLOOMING FORWARD

Gratitude isn't reserved for calm seasons or easy mornings. It's something we choose and nurture—even when the ground beneath us feels unsteady. Gratitude doesn't deny what's broken; it dares to say, *"There is something here worth honoring."* I've come to see it as a kind of emotional clarity—a way of looking at life through what remains, not only what was lost. The more we practice noticing what is still good, the more its meaning deepens. Gratitude may not change our circumstances, but it changes us. It softens hard edges, steadies us in uncertainty, and roots us in the present.

Look closely at your life—not just the highlights, but the moments you may overlook because they feel ordinary. The first bloom of spring. The text that says, "Just checking on you." The steady rhythm of your breath. These aren't small things; they are proof that life is still moving through you. Beauty is woven into the rhythm of your days.

As Melody Beattie wrote, *"Gratitude unlocks the fullness of life. It turns what we have into enough, and more."* Gratitude doesn't ask for perfection; it asks for presence. When we stop rushing past blessings we think are too small to count, we discover how abundant our lives really are.

One of the most transformative shifts for me came when I began saying "thank you" in the middle of my questions. I didn't wait for healing to be complete or for every answer to arrive. I thanked God for the strength to endure, for resilience I didn't know I had, and for mercies that carried me on my hardest days. That simple act—acknowledging what was holding me when I couldn't hold myself—reframed everything.

Philippians 4:6 (NIV) reminds us, *"Do not be anxious about anything, but in every situation, by prayer and petition, with thanksgiving, present your requests to God."* Gratitude isn't an afterthought once the breakthrough comes; it's what carries us through the unknown. The more we carry it, the more it opens our eyes to grace.

That's the exchange: gratitude helps us notice grace, and grace gives us even more to be thankful for. One flows into the other until they are inseparable. Gratitude grounds us in the now, while grace lifts us into what's next.

And when I bake now—stirring spices, smoothing batter into the pan—I sometimes think of my grandmother's kitchen. How the sweetness of her pies seemed to carry more than flavor; it carried memory, endurance, and love. Gratitude feels like that too. A quiet recipe passed down through generations. A reminder that what we create, nurture, and give thanks for doesn't end with us—it continues through every life we touch.

So here's your invitation: slow down long enough to notice. Let today be the day you name the goodness around you, however subtle it may be. Light a candle and give thanks for what you've survived. Speak a blessing over your own life—over the version of you still learning, healing, and believing. Write down one thing you're grateful for and let that single thread lead you to more.

Gratitude doesn't need a spotlight. It simply asks for your heart, open and honest. And when you answer its question—*What beauty lives here, even now?*—you're not just giving thanks. You're anchoring yourself in grace. And that anchor will hold.

CHAPTER 17
Extending Grace to Others

There comes a moment in the healing journey when the grace you've been learning to give yourself begins to ask for movement beyond you. That's where it gets tender. It's one thing to forgive yourself for what you didn't know back then; it's another to extend that same softness to those who hurt you—especially when they've never asked for it or still can't see the harm they caused.

Extending grace is not about excusing what they did. It's about choosing not to carry the weight of it forever. It's saying, *I will not let what you did define how I love, how I trust, or how I move through this life.* For a long time, I mistook forgiveness for pretending it didn't matter—or letting people back in who had already shown they couldn't hold my heart well. Over time I learned that grace and boundaries are not enemies; they work together. Releasing someone doesn't erase what happened. It simply means choosing healing over harboring.

I've forgiven people silently—those who will never know the depth of the wounds they left. I've also had to walk away from others out of self-respect. Grace gave me the courage to stop waiting for apologies and reclaim peace anyway. The hardest person to extend it to is often the one who mirrors your own missteps: a parent who abandoned you, a friend who betrayed you, or the version of yourself who hurt someone else. Grace doesn't excuse harm; it helps us see that pain is often passed down, not born in isolation.

Freedom begins when we stop expecting perfection—from others or ourselves. Extending grace means refusing to define people by their worst moment. It says, *I see your humanity, even when I can't have you close.* This kind of grace transforms everything. It makes space for others to grow, even if you never witness it. It lets you bless and release without bitterness, allowing healing to speak louder than hurt. There is quiet strength in saying, *I wish you well, even from afar.*

Offering grace is more than politeness; it's a conscious decision to meet the world with patience and compassion when every impulse says protect yourself. It looks like listening without judgment, forgiving without fanfare, and offering support without expectation. Grace is not weakness—it is power under control, the steady strength to rise above frustration or resentment.

Grace can also build bridges where walls once stood. In relationships, it restores trust and makes connection possible again. Think of a time someone extended grace to you—maybe they forgave a mistake you thought would end everything, or showed gentleness when you expected anger. That act did more than ease tension; it expanded your sense of belonging. To receive grace is to be reminded that love can still live in broken places.

Still, grace does not always require proximity. You can forgive someone and still choose not to grant them access to your most tender spaces. That isn't pettiness—it's wisdom. Grace isn't about letting someone wound you again in the name of love; it's discernment in action. I've released people without a single conversation, not because they earned it, but because I needed space for joy, clarity, and peace. As long as bitterness sat at the table of my heart, nothing else could grow.

Grace entered slowly—through tears, through prayer, through time—and when it finally settled, I realized something important: extending grace doesn't just free them. It frees me.

That freedom often begins with empathy. When we make the effort to understand another perspective, compassion grows even in hard soil. Empathy reminds us that everyone carries unseen battles. It doesn't justify harm, but it softens our response. It opens the door to grace.

Empathy deepens through intentional listening. When someone shares their truth, try to hear them fully—without preparing your defense or framing a rebuttal. Let them feel seen. Hold back judgment. Their choices may have been shaped by pain you'll never witness. Instead of rushing to conclusions, pause and ask, *What might they be facing that I don't understand?* That practice doesn't erase hurt, but it stretches the heart and allows room for healing.

I once believed grace had to be mutual—that I could only offer it if the other person came back ready to repair what was broken. It felt fair, even righteous. But life doesn't always offer that symmetry. Some people never return. Some never apologize. Some never see what they did.

And still, grace asks the deeper question: *Will you release them anyway?* Not to absolve them, but to let your own soul breathe again.

Forgiveness is one of the deepest expressions of grace. It doesn't rewrite history or minimize pain; it simply releases the need to keep reliving it. Forgiveness is a gift—not only for them but for you.

Begin gently. Write about what happened. Name what still lingers. Then ask, *What am I ready to let go of so I can move forward?* Sometimes forgiveness looks like unclenching a fist. Sometimes it's releasing anger piece by piece. It rarely happens in a single moment. What matters is staying open to peace.

Remembering how God has extended grace to me humbles me—not because I always got it right, but because I was willing to grow. Even in my missteps, grace came. That reminder steadies me now. I no longer wait for perfect apologies. Permission to walk in peace is already mine.

When I say, *I see what happened. I accept the truth of it. And I will not chain myself to it anymore,* I am choosing grace. That is an act of holy rebellion. The world teaches us to harden, to match energy, to repay harm with harm. But we are not called to mirror brokenness; we are called to transform it.

I imagine grace as a circle drawn around me—not permission, but protection. Inside that circle, I am free to live soft again, to laugh again, to trust again. Grace doesn't cancel grief; it holds it tenderly until it loosens its grip. Some relationships may never be restored, and that's okay. Forgiveness and reconciliation are different paths. One releases; the other rebuilds. Sometimes the healthier choice is to let the bond change form—or end altogether—without bitterness. Peace can exist even when closeness cannot.

Grace is both boundary and balm in motion. You can love someone and still love them from afar. You can forgive without forgetting, honoring what was while honoring yourself more. One of the most profound acts of grace is releasing the version of you who stayed in survival mode because she didn't know how to let go. You are not her anymore. You don't have to carry it all to prove your worth. You are allowed to grow, to bloom, to extend grace, and to guard your peace.

Grace rarely arrives in grand gestures. It lives in small choices—a kind word, a patient pause, a breath taken before you react. These everyday mercies move grace from concept to practice.

If someone's name still stings when it surfaces, ask yourself, *What would it look like to offer grace without reopening the wound?* Maybe it's lighting a candle and whispering a prayer over their name. Maybe it's writing what you wish they had said and deciding not to wait for it anymore. Maybe it's closing the door gently, not with anger but with release: *I let you go. I let me go. I choose freedom.*

At its core, grace is a return to peace. It doesn't always come wrapped in apologies. Sometimes it comes as release—the quiet courage to stop carrying what was never yours to hold.

And as the journey continues, the next question arises: after extending grace to others, can you extend it to yourself? In the next chapter, we'll step into that stillness—the part of healing that doesn't demand action but invites rest. You don't need closure to choose peace. You don't have to stay tangled in old wounds to prove they mattered. Extending grace—especially to those who may never know they needed it—is not about forgetting what happened. It's about making space for what still can be.

BLOOMING FORWARD

Letting go doesn't mean pretending the pain never happened. It means refusing to let it live rent-free in your spirit. Grace in action is the decision to stop rehearsing the hurt and start reclaiming your peace. You can honor your story and still choose freedom. You can say, *Yes, it mattered—and still, I will not be defined by it.* Grace doesn't erase the past; it simply reminds you that the past no longer has the final say.

It took me years to learn that peace isn't something others hand you; it's a gift you give yourself. Not out of pride, but purpose. Not to let someone off the hook, but to finally stop waiting on acknowledgment that may never come. You can bless someone from afar without inviting them back into your inner circle. That boundary isn't bitterness—it's wisdom, dignity, and self-trust.

Grace also makes room for empathy, the kind that doesn't excuse harm but dares to see the fuller story. It asks you to consider what shaped another's choices—not to justify, but to release yourself from carrying their brokenness as if it were yours. When anger rises or grief returns, grace helps you pause. It helps you breathe. It reminds you that you are not your pain and you no longer have to participate in cycles that keep you small. There is liberation in refusing to harden.

When the world tells you to build walls, grace invites you to draw a circle wide enough to hold your healing, your joy, and maybe—someday—your forgiveness. Not because they earned it, but because you deserve it.

Mark Nepo once wrote, "The pain was necessary to know the truth, but we don't have to keep the pain alive to keep the truth alive... Forgiveness has deeper rewards than excusing someone for how they hurt us. The deeper healing comes in the exchange of our resentments for inner freedom." That is what grace makes possible: a love that doesn't need perfection to be powerful, a love that knows when to stay soft and when to stand firm. Grace allows you to release the story without losing the lesson, to turn the page without burning the book, to keep your heart open without leaving the door unlocked.

As Colossians 3:13 (NIV) reminds us, *"Bear with each other and forgive one another if any of you has a grievance against someone. Forgive as the Lord forgave you."* That is the invitation—not to forget what was done, but to walk forward with less weight and more wisdom.

So if a name rises in your spirit, if a memory still aches, ask yourself: *Can I offer grace—not to excuse, but to be free?* Grace comes in many forms. However it arrives, let it come gently, honestly, and with the kind of love that says: *I release this not because it didn't matter, but because I do.*

CHAPTER 18
The Echo of His Absence

S ome stories live in your bones—stories that shape not only how you see the world but how you see yourself. My story with love, trust, and what it means to feel safe in connection begins with one person: my biological father.

He wasn't absent in the traditional sense. I knew him. I spent time with him. Yet his presence always felt like an echo—close enough to hear, never close enough to hold. He battled alcoholism for most of his life, a disease tangled with other struggles that kept him from being the father I needed or deserved. Still, I loved him. Always. And that love often wrestled with something harder to admit—disappointment.

Earlier in the book, I shared how I used to dream the Incredible Hulk would show up and rescue me. To some it might sound odd, but when you're a child longing for a hero, you cling to anything that feels strong enough to break through the chaos. What I really wanted was for my father to be that hero—to show up, take my hand, and choose me. But he didn't. Or maybe he couldn't.

Our relationship was complicated—filled with silent longings, aching gaps, and moments that never lived up to what I needed them to be. Yes, I knew him. Yes, we spent time together. But the man I needed—the present, protective, emotionally available father I deserved—never fully showed up. At times, he was physically there, but the connection was like smoke: visible, impossible to hold.

He faced his own inner battles, shaped by trauma I would only come to understand later. He served in the military, and according to my grandmother—his mother—something in him shifted after his service. She would say, "They don't treat Black soldiers right in this country. Something happened to your daddy while he was serving." Whether it was mistreatment, pressure, or a deeper wound that affected him, I may never fully know. What I do know is that many of the men in our family—faced similar demons. And those battles often left the next generation to pick up the pieces.

For years, I wrestled with the duality of loving my father and resenting him at the same time. I loved him because I was his daughter. I wanted him to be proud of me, to show up like other fathers did. Yet I also carried the weight of his absence—every missed birthday, every milestone he didn't witness, every moment I silently wished he would change his mind and be a constant in my life. That tug-of-war between longing and disappointment lived deep in my spirit.

My grandmother tried to explain. "Baby," she told me when I was young, "I've tried. I've begged your daddy to be better. But I can't make him be a man. I can't make any of my sons do right. But I'm your grand momma, and your grand momma don't have much, but whatever I have is yours." And she meant it. She poured her love into me like an offering, an apology for all that was missing. She baked my favorite sweet potato pie and southern dishes when I visited. She mailed birthday cards every year without fail. She listened to my dreams and said, "If that's what you want, baby, you can do it. You can be it." She believed in me, even when I doubted myself.

There's a story in our family—one I cherish—about the first time she laid eyes on me. After finding out her youngest son had gotten my mother pregnant, she marched to my maternal grandmother's house, knocked on the door, and said, "I hear I got a grandbaby here, and I want to see my grandbaby." That story has stayed with me all these years, not just because it makes me smile, but because it reminds me that I've always been worth showing up for, even when not everyone did.

When I learned that my father was battling not only alcoholism but also cancer, I spent time with him at his home. We discovered a few things we had in common: our love for old Westerns, our enjoyment of singing, our sense of humor. For the first time, I felt like we weren't just strangers bound by blood. I watched him soften in those final days, and though the years couldn't be undone, there was something healing about that season.

One day at the hospital, as I sat by his bedside, I asked the question that had lived in my heart for years: "Why couldn't you be a father to me?" He didn't say much. He just looked at me with tired eyes and said, "I would've just messed your life up. You wouldn't be the woman you are if I'd been there." Then he shut down.

The truth is, his answer stung. He never knew the full extent of what I endured, or how his presence might have changed the course of my life—or prevented some of the harm. In that moment, I could have pushed, argued, demanded more. But what was I supposed to do? Debate with a man on his deathbed? As a daughter, and as a human being, I chose to give him peace from my end. Whatever he had to atone for would remain his to carry. Part of me was still disappointed, still his, but I also knew I could not stay there forever.

I'll never know the whole story of the battles he fought—what the military took from him, or what demons followed him home. Those pieces are not mine to solve, and I have learned not to spend my life trying to decipher another person's choices or silences.

He passed away on January 15—Dr. Martin Luther King Jr.'s birthday. It feels symbolic now, like he left this world on a day that also represents legacy, struggle, and the pursuit of something better. The last time I saw him, he was angry at me and my aunt. He wanted to go home, to live out his final days in our care, but the doctors said it wasn't safe. He didn't understand that. When I said goodbye, he was upset—his memory already fading, his perception shifting. I looked at him and said, "I love you, Dad. And I forgive you." I knew in my soul it would be the last time. He died days later.

What I have left of my father lives in both the material and the unseen. I still have the U.S. flag that was laid across his casket during the funeral, a solemn reminder of the life he lived and the service he gave. I have his old hat rack, the one that held his beloved hats, each brim a small reflection of his style and pride. I also have notebooks from his time in Alcoholics Anonymous, pages filled with his handwriting—apologies not directed to any one person but words that seemed to reach toward God, asking for forgiveness. I have photographs that trace his life through different seasons, capturing his stance, his smirk, and most of all, his beautiful brown eyes, a mixture of brandy and honey. He often wore shades, so glimpses of them were rare, but when you caught them, it was unforgettable. His eyes carried a depth the world could not erase.

Beyond what I can hold in my hands, I carry what cannot be boxed or stored away. I carry his fight. His resilience. Certain angles of my face still remind me of him, as if his features were etched into mine as a quiet inheritance. And most of all, I carry him as an angel now—no longer bound by his battles, but present in a way I can receive without fear of disappointment.

For years, I used to blame my grandmother, wondering why she couldn't make her son be the man I needed. But over time, I came to understand that love, even in its most powerful form, cannot make someone change. People choose their paths, and sometimes those paths lead them away from the ones who need them most. My grandmother did everything she could, and I will always honor her for that. In fact, my pen name—Rose—is in honor of her. She was one of my greatest gifts.

My father and grandmother died within a year of each other—she in 2016, he in 2017. His spirit was so tethered to hers that I believe if cancer hadn't taken him, grief would have. He was a mother's boy to the end. I carry pieces of both of them with me.

This story isn't just about grief. It's about love in its most imperfect, tangled form. About longing for someone who may never fully meet you where you are and learning how to make peace with that. And it's about breaking cycles while holding compassion for the people who were caught in them. Ultimately, it's about choosing to release what wasn't so you can make room for what is.

I may not have had the father I needed, but I became the woman I was meant to be. And that, in its own way, is redemption.

Though my biological father's absence left wounds that ran deep, I was blessed to experience the other side of fatherhood through my stepfather—a man who, in many ways, gave me the chance to be a daddy's girl. He stepped in when the weight of life felt unbearable, when silence felt too loud. He showed up in ways I didn't always know how to ask for. And while he couldn't erase the ache left behind, he offered me something I never thought I'd have—a safe space to lean into softness, to be protected, and to be seen. He reminded me, through his quiet strength, that love could be steady.

Later, I began to trace the emotional residue of my father's absence into the patterns of my own relationships. In my late teens and early twenties, I experienced what many would call young, innocent love—the kind that blooms when everything still feels possible. And yet, both of those relationships echoed something deeper I hadn't yet healed: the ache of being left behind.

The first relationship felt like a sweet beginning. He was a little older, ahead of me in school, and soon he made the decision to join the military. That one decision—though it had nothing to do with me—triggered something I hadn't expected. Suddenly I was the high school girl watching someone I loved move on, not just with his life but with his identity. I imagined the future: him meeting new people, older women, more experienced and worldly. And there I was—frozen in place, afraid of being forgotten. So, I made the move first. I ended things. Not because I stopped caring, but because I didn't believe I could ask him to stay. And he didn't stop me. He didn't fight for me. That quiet exit, that slow letting go, whispered the same story my younger heart had always known: they leave.

The second relationship cut even deeper. It was a wild ride—full of passion, emotion, ups and downs. I tried to stand by his side through it all, to hold it down, to be his anchor. I poured into him, gave pieces of myself freely, hoping love would be enough to hold us both together. But I didn't yet understand that he was still trying to figure out who he was, while I—because of what I had lived through—had already been forced to grow up too fast. My expectations, my emotional bandwidth, the ways I showed up in that relationship—they were all shaped by survival. I was loving from a place that demanded maturity he hadn't yet reached. And still, the love was there. That part was never a question.

He, too, chose the military. And suddenly, just like before, I was the one left standing still while someone I loved walked away. It was abandonment all over again—but this time, it wasn't just about him. It was about the story I carried in my spirit. My father had gone to the military and left my mother behind. And now here I was, again, with another man putting on a uniform and disappearing into a future that didn't include me. At least that's what my heart believed.

I remember confiding in a close friend about both of those relationships, the ones I couldn't seem to move past. She looked at me and said something I'll never forget: "Those boys loved you. I used to watch them watching you. You couldn't fake that. They really loved you." And maybe they did. But love, unspoken or unmet, can still leave you feeling abandoned. And when that feeling already lives in your bones, even the sincerest love can still hurt like rejection.

Those experiences taught me something I didn't have the language for back then: not everyone who leaves is trying to hurt you. And not every departure is about your worth. Sometimes people are just trying to find themselves. Sometimes they're carrying their own unhealed wounds. But when your foundation has been shaped by the ache of not being chosen, it's hard to see the difference.

And just when I thought the relationship had run its course, when I thought it would fade into memory like so many others, he surprised me. He asked me to marry him. He gave me a ring—tangible proof that, in his heart, he saw a future with me. That moment should have felt like a fairytale. But instead, I froze. I couldn't say yes. Not because I didn't care for him—because I did. But something deeper beneath my hesitation still lived unhealed.

I was still in foster care, still holding onto dreams of finishing college, of becoming something, someone. I didn't want to leave my mother behind. More than that, I didn't trust the opportunity it presented. I didn't trust the idea that something good could be meant for me. Traveling the world, building a life, stepping into love that big—it felt like too much. Like a dream meant for someone else.

And maybe, just maybe, I didn't trust him to carry me. To protect me. To make me feel safe. My heart had been trained to survive, not to soften into someone else's care. I had built a life around self-reliance, contingency plans, and backup exits. Saying yes would have meant surrendering some of that control. It would have meant trusting that this time, someone would stay. And I didn't know how to believe in that kind of security—not yet.

Looking back, I realize that moment wasn't just about a proposal. It was about everything I was still carrying: the fear of being abandoned, the wounds of being left to figure it out alone, the need to prove I could make it on my own. Saying no wasn't about him. It was about protecting the part of me that had been disappointed too many times to trust what felt too good to be true.

Even so, there's something tender in remembering that I was loved. Even when I couldn't receive it fully and I couldn't say yes.

There were beautiful moments, too. The first boy, as I mentioned, was older than me, already working a part-time job while finishing high school. Almost every payday, without fail, he bought me roses—roses of every color. Red. Yellow. Orange. Sometimes pink. He did it without prompting, without fanfare. It was his way of seeing me, of honoring me, even if he never said the words aloud. And I remember holding those roses with such care. No one had ever made me feel that special without strings attached.

That kind of love—young, unfiltered, sweet—left an imprint. Even now, I can still see those flowers in my mind, their petals bold and bright against whatever storm was passing through my life at the time. They reminded me that love didn't always come to break me. Sometimes it arrived gently, unexpectedly, like a soft thing in a harsh world.

There are some sounds in life that stay with you forever, sounds that soothe you, ground you—like the ocean, a favorite childhood song, or the rustle of wind through trees. The second guy's voice was like that for me. A gentle breeze. Not loud or commanding, but familiar, steady, safe. Hearing it reminded me of a version of myself I sometimes forgot—a version still capable of softness, of joy, of ease. Some people have a way of calling you back to yourself. He was one of them.

But when those relationships ended—especially the second one, the one that carried my hopes a little further—I changed. Something hardened in me. I started building a wall. Not out of bitterness, but out of survival. I became the girl who wouldn't let her guard down easily, who didn't let anyone get too close too fast. Because when someone leaves, even if they love you, it still feels like abandonment. And I had been abandoned too many times.

Looking back, I can admit I wasn't just on the receiving end of heartbreak—I caused some of it, too. I made choices from a place of fear, insecurity, and the inability to trust love without expecting pain. And in doing so, I hurt people who genuinely cared for me. That's a hard truth to hold, but it's one I've made peace with.

Time has a way of offering clarity. I've reflected deeply on the girl I was back then—how she showed up, how she protected herself, how she sometimes pushed love away even while longing for it. And I've forgiven her. I've forgiven myself. For the walls I built, for the goodbyes I didn't explain, for the chances I couldn't take, for the choices I made. It was all part of my becoming.

What brings me peace is knowing we all went on to live full, meaningful lives. We found our paths. We became the people we were always meant to be. And maybe that's the most beautiful ending of all—not a fairytale, not a return to what was, but a quiet release and a mutual rising.

Maybe that's why this chapter in my life feels less like a clean ending and more like a release. Not a forgetting, but a setting down of what was never mine to hold. And in that letting go, space opened—for healing, for gratitude, and for the kind of love that stays.

BLOOMING FORWARD

There comes a moment in healing when you stop asking why someone couldn't love you the way you needed and begin recognizing how deeply you've learned to love yourself. That moment doesn't always arrive with clarity. More often, it slips in quietly—through small acts of self-compassion, through choosing peace on an ordinary day, through realizing your worth was never tethered to another person's ability to stay. The ache of absence—especially from someone meant to protect you—can echo for years. But even echoes fade. Even grief softens. Over time, you begin to fill those once-empty spaces with your own voice, your own strength, your own love.

What carries you forward isn't perfection or certainty—it's presence. It's showing up for yourself in ways others could not. Allowing yourself to grieve and forgive in the same breath. It's choosing peace not because it erases pain, but because it makes room to hope, to keep becoming. Along the way you discover your story was never defined by abandonment. It has always been unfolding in resilience, carrying you even when you couldn't see the way.

Writer Amanda Ripley once said, "Resilience is a precious skill. People who have it have three advantages: a belief they can influence life events, a tendency to find meaning and purpose in life's turmoil, and a conviction they can learn from positive and negative experiences." That truth is alive in you. Even when love felt confusing, even when silence screamed louder than presence, you didn't stop hoping. You didn't stop learning or loving—even when love had to be rebuilt through tears, boundaries, and courage no one else could measure but you.

And when you felt most alone, you were not truly abandoned. Scripture reminds us in Psalm 34:18 (NIV): "The Lord is close to the brokenhearted and saves those who are crushed in spirit." Every tear you cried was seen. Every longing you carried was held. Every breaking point became a threshold into deeper strength. You were not unchosen; you were deeply known.

So here is the invitation: release the story that someone else's absence defines your value. Let go of the weight of *what could have been* so your hands are free to receive what still can be. Bless the younger you who did the best she could with what she had and honor the woman you are now—the one who knows how to love without losing herself. Build a life that does not demand proof, only presence. Live with a love that steadies, protects peace, and honors truth.

You are not too much. You are not too late. You are never too hard to love. Life's trials and tribulations may have shaped you, but they did not silence you. Your voice rises now in truth, healing, and freedom. And that's the kind of love that stays.

As grace settles into the heart, something shifts. The grief that once felt heavy begins to guide instead of haunt. Purpose starts to bloom quietly through the cracks—through healing, through truth, through the courage to keep showing up whole. What once felt like loss becomes direction. What once silenced you becomes your voice. Every fragment of pain, every layer of grace, has been leading you here—to the steady unfolding of who you were always meant to become.

PART FOUR: THE JOURNEY TO ME

*"I have fallen in love with the imagination.
And if you fall in love with the imagination,
you understand that it is a free spirit."*
— Alice Walker

CHAPTER 19
The Authentic Self

There's a certain kind of loneliness that comes from not living as your *whole* self—when pieces of who you are stay tucked away until trust feels safe enough to open. You can sit among people who love you, laugh with you, hear them call you "strong," even celebrate your accomplishments—and still feel unseen. When only parts of you are seen or celebrated, every cheer feels a little hollow. I lived that way for years—smiling in photos while my eyes looked tired, showing up to events I didn't want to attend, saying yes when my soul was shouting no. The hardest part was learning how to let the rest of me be seen.

It's possible to love your life and still feel invisible. You can be grateful for your blessings, proud of your progress, and still sense a quiet ache beneath it all. That doesn't mean you're ungrateful—it means something within you is asking to be witnessed. Sometimes invisibility isn't about others overlooking you; it's about losing sight of yourself in the rhythm of responsibility. You can have purpose and still feel unseen when your inner world goes unheard. Authenticity begins in that moment—the decision to see yourself fully, even before anyone else does.

Truth doesn't stay buried forever. It rises, even when we try to press it down. For me, it surfaced in small ways. I could no longer tolerate certain conversations. I grew uneasy in rooms where I once blended easily. Solitude began calling me. Silence. The sound of my own voice, unfiltered.

Authenticity isn't about perfection or preference—it's about alignment. It's the harmony between who you are, what you believe, and how you live.

That kind of alignment carries a cost. Relationships built on quiet compliance may fall away. Jobs that once defined you lose their hold. People accustomed to the gentler version of you might not understand your growth. But what you gain? You gain yourself. Days rooted in peace instead of performance. Friendships that see the real you and stay—not in spite of your complexity, but because of your honesty. Peace that settles into your bones. And most importantly, trust in yourself again.

For a long time, I thought my intuition had gone dormant. I feared I could no longer hear from God, from Spirit, from myself. The truth was simpler: I had stopped listening. I drowned out the stillness with noise. Once I sat in the quiet, I realized I had not lost my way—I had been walking someone else's path. Pressures, expectations, and survival strategies push us to conform, sometimes at the cost of our wholeness. Over time, choices made to fit in or avoid judgment distance us from who we were created to be.

The process of letting go doesn't just strip away titles—it reawakens memory. Sometimes what falls away uncovers what once brought you joy. Think back to childhood, before outside voices shaped your steps. What brought you joy then? Drawing, singing, building, exploring? Those early passions often carry clues to your authentic self—the unfiltered, joyful version of you. Rediscovering what once lit your heart is one way to reconnect with who you are beneath the layers.

When you begin honoring your truth—the deep, imperfect, evolving truth—you feel it. A softness returns. Laughter grows louder. Steps feel lighter. Your "no" gains strength. Tears no longer feel shameful; they become reminders of tenderness. Even on hard days, you stop feeling like a stranger to yourself. Because you're home. And home isn't a place—it's a return to the woman God always knew you to be.

Peeling back layers requires courage. It means removing the protective coverings built for survival and allowing yourself to be seen. Vulnerability becomes part of the process. Each time I told the truth—about what I needed, what I feared, or what I could no longer carry—I risked misunderstanding. Yet every honest moment built a bridge back to myself. A helpful practice is to list five things you love because they bring joy. Reflect on what makes you feel inspired and at peace. These moments are guideposts. They reveal what matters most and where you feel most like yourself.

There's a tenderness in telling the truth about who you are—not the polished version for approval, but the soul-deep truth of the you that shows up when no one is watching. She may stumble over words or second-guess her choices. She may carry scars that ache when it rains. But she's real. And that realness heals.

Individuality is a gift. Every quirk, passion, and trait forms a part of who you are. Embracing genuineness means celebrating what makes you unique and recognizing that your difference is your strength. Affirmations can help anchor this truth:

I am enough, exactly as I am. My difference is my divine design. I honor my truth and live from it daily.

Living authentically isn't about flawlessness—it's about integrity. When you live in your truth, self-expression expands, confidence grows, and fulfillment follows. You no longer need to audition for your own life. That realization came to me one quiet day at my kitchen table. I had spent years chasing purpose, chasing people, chasing peace—while neglecting the parts of myself that needed care: my joy, my boundaries, my softness, even my laughter.

The authentic self is the version of you that existed before shame took root, when worth wasn't measured by what you gave or how little you needed. It was the time before love grew conditional, before silence became a strategy for safety. She's still there—still waiting, still whole. Reconnecting with her doesn't demand perfection. It asks only for permission.

Living authentically takes courage, especially in the face of misunderstanding or rejection. Fear of judgment can make us retreat, but the truth remains: the opinions of others do not define you. Your worth lies in living from the core of who you are, even when it feels vulnerable.

When fear rises, return to your values. Ask yourself, *Am I living in alignment with what I believe?* When your choices flow from conviction, the opinions of others lose their hold. Surround yourself with people who make it safe to be fully seen. Celebrate each act of bravery—every choice to show up as yourself, even when it feels risky. That is courage in motion.

Create your own authentic blueprint—a mission statement that reflects your values, passions, and definition of truth. Write what matters most. Identify what brings joy, fulfillment, and purpose. Capture it in a few sentences as a reminder to live honestly and intentionally. For example: *I strive to live a life rooted in kindness, creativity, and growth. I celebrate my uniqueness and honor my true self in every choice I make.* That blueprint becomes a compass for your journey home.

Authenticity, when rooted in faith, becomes devotion—a daily practice of choosing truth over approval. The invitation of authenticity is not simply to feel seen—it is to feel whole. To live so rooted in truth that you stop shrinking for spaces never meant to hold you. When you align your choices, your voice, and your presence with the woman God designed, something shifts. Performance falls away. Becoming begins. Survival loosens its grip. Creation takes root.

Authenticity doesn't just set you free—it clears the way for purpose.

BLOOMING FORWARD

Sometimes the hardest part isn't figuring out who you are—it's giving yourself permission to live as her, fully and unapologetically. The world hands us scripts and roles to perform, as if they were woven into our DNA. When we're not careful, worth gets measured by how seamlessly we perform instead of how deeply we feel at peace. Authenticity begins the moment those scripts are laid down. It starts when the question shifts from "Who do they need me to be?" to "Who am I when I feel free?" Living authentically is rarely about reinvention; more often, it's about returning—coming back to the joy that once made your eyes shine. Reclaiming the version of you who laughed without glancing for approval. Holding onto what felt right before it ever needed to make sense to anyone else.

There is a joy that comes only when performance ends and presence takes its place. As pressure loosens, life begins to reflect your values instead of your survival strategies. Being real carries risks. Some people may feel disappointed when the edited version of you fades away. Some spaces that once felt like home may no longer welcome your truth. Yet what comes in return is alignment—a sense of wholeness that cannot be manufactured. Your voice begins to sound like your own again. The mirror shows a reflection that feels familiar. Each "yes" carries integrity rather than compromise. The journey may not be seamless, but every step will be worth it.

E. E. Cummings once wrote, "The hardest challenge is to be yourself in a world where everyone is trying to make you be somebody else." Choosing authenticity remains one of the most resilient acts available. It calls us to listen to our lives and to shift course when our soul whispers, *This no longer fits.* Fear may disguise itself as logic, and doubt may insist that the truest version of you is too much or not enough. Still, truth affirmed by God stands steady.

You were never asked to shrink to be worthy of love. You were never called to perform to belong. Galatians 1:10 (NIV) reminds us: *"Am I now trying to win the approval of human beings, or of God? Or am I trying to please people? If I were still trying to please people, I would not be a servant of Christ."* That reminder anchors us. The more honesty we practice with ourselves, the less we long for validation that demands pretense.

So today, return to yourself—not the curated image the world applauds, not the edited version that feels safe in every room. Return to the whole and unguarded you—the woman God saw and loved before the world misnamed her. She is not just enough; she is essential. Living from her truth is how you reclaim your life and light the path for others.

CHAPTER 20
Beauty, Reclaimed

I don't remember the exact moment I realized the world saw me differently than I saw myself. But I remember the shift—when the mirror became a battleground. When the soft, girly identity my mother wrapped around me like a blanket began to unravel under the weight of other people's opinions.

As a little girl, I believed I was beautiful because my mother told me so. She dressed me in bright colors, outfits full of character. To anyone who would listen she'd say, "Victoria is a pretty girl. Look at those big, beautiful eyes." One of my uncles nicknamed me "Lady," not only for how I looked but for the way I carried myself—prissy, gentle, polished. My stepfather echoed those words. Between them, I was built up to believe I was lovely and special.

That's the story I held onto—until the world decided to interrupt it.

I remember sitting in a room full of kids and adults watching *The Color Purple*. Desreta Jackson and Whoopi Goldberg played young and grown Celie; Akosua Busia was her sister,

Nettie. During one scene someone said, "Victoria is Celie, and Tanya is Nettie." The laughter that followed said more than the words ever could. Then someone pointed out the difference between our hair textures—hers longer and softer-wavy, mine thick and coily. The comment hung in the air like a quiet comparison, and something inside me shifted.

Suddenly, my expressive eyes weren't beautiful—they were "pop-eyed." My rich skin tone wasn't regal—it was "tar baby" dark. Years later a childhood friend told me, "You finally grew into your nose." Each remark lodged like a pebble under the skin. My heart sank as I caught sight of my reflection, my eyes suddenly feeling like a target instead of a window to my soul. The world often tries to sand down our edges, mistaking our distinction for something that needs correction.

But let me be clear: I never stopped loving my big brown eyes. I always thought they were bold, soulful, and full of story. Even when others tried to convince me otherwise, something in me refused to hand over that truth.

Still, I would be lying if I said those words didn't plant seeds—doubt, comparison, confusion. For a season, I critiqued my own reflection: my eyes, my nose, my skin, my lips. Wondering if I was missing something. Wondering if I needed to change.

But something else rose up in me too.

I remembered every compliment my mother gave me, every time she said "Be beautiful" before hanging up the phone. I heard her voice reminding me that beauty was more than skin deep—that it fades, that it can be crushed under the weight of a hard-lived life. I thought of women I admired—icons, artists, and everyday heroines— who shared my features, who moved through the world with grace and quiet confidence. Women like Diana Ross, Toni Braxton, Sade, and Janet Jackson, whose poise reminded me that femininity could be soft and powerful at once. And women like Lauryn Hill, Gabrielle Union, and Nia Long, who carried the kind of radiance that felt familiar—a beauty rooted in confidence, not conformity.

That's when I made the decision to reclaim what the world tried to take.

Because here's what I've learned: we don't know anything is "wrong" with us until someone tells us there is—until society draws its small boxes around what is acceptable, worthy, or beautiful. And when we're young, still forming our sense of self, those labels cling like glue. They shape how we move, how we hide, how we perform for the sake of approval.

But we were never meant to perform our worth.

I had to teach myself that the opinions of others were never meant to be the standard I measured myself against. How I saw myself—what I believed about myself—was the fuel that powered everything. And I had a choice: accept the perceptions handed to me by people who didn't truly see me, or look into the mirror and remember who I've always been.

The truth is, this world has been cruel to girls who look like me—to girls with deep melanin, wide features, and hair that defies gravity. It tries to rewrite us. But we don't have to accept that narrative. Because I've seen what happens when a woman reclaims the pen.

I've seen what happens when she turns down the volume of the outside world and tunes in to the still, inner knowing within herself. When she stops trying to earn love by shrinking or softening her brilliance. When she claims her beauty simply by existing—and no one gets to define that but her.

That moment watching *The Color Purple* could have scarred me permanently. And maybe it did, in a way. Maybe it left a mark. But it also sparked awareness—how early the world begins assigning value based on proximity to a beauty standard most of us were never meant to fit, and how powerful it is when we decide we don't need to fit in. We were born to stand out.

So yes, there were times I doubted. Times I questioned. Times I looked at someone else and thought, *Maybe if I looked more like her...* But those moments were fleeting. They never defined me.

What defined me was my return.

My return to that little girl my mother called beautiful. My return to the knowing that I am soft and strong and special. That my beauty is not up for debate. That I don't have to prove anything to anyone.

The lesson I hope you take from this chapter is simple but life-changing: you lose your power the moment you let someone else define your worth. And your power is too precious to give away.

You are already enough. You are already a masterpiece. The world doesn't get to rewrite that—not with its comments, not with its laughter, not with its ignorance. Reclaim your mirror. Reclaim your truth. Walk boldly in the beauty that is uniquely, undeniably yours.

BLOOMING FORWARD

There's power in reclaiming your reflection—not just the one in the mirror, but the one you carry in memory. For many of us, the earliest messages about beauty didn't come wrapped in love; they arrived through comparison, cruelty, or silence.

Over time, those messages sink so deeply that we forget how to see ourselves clearly. We measure our worth against someone else's standard, or worse, dim our light to avoid judgment. But beauty was never meant to be assigned by popular vote; it was meant to be lived from the inside out.

Helen Keller once said, "Character cannot be developed in ease and quiet. Only through experience of trial and suffering can the soul be strengthened, ambition inspired, and success achieved." Her words remind me that reflection isn't only about appearance—it's shaped by the resilience built through every trial endured. Beauty, then, is not just what's visible. It's what's survived.

Maybe no one ever told you that your nose was regal, your skin radiant, your eyes poetic. Maybe you were taught to soften your features so others would feel comfortable. But what if today you began telling a new story? What if the mirror became a place of reunion instead of rejection—a space where you remind yourself you are already enough? Not someday. Not after a transformation. Not when you meet a certain size or style. But right now, exactly as you are.

And when rising feels heavy—when the voice of criticism echoes louder than your own—hold on to this truth: *"You are altogether beautiful, my darling; there is no flaw in you"* (Song of Songs 4:7, NIV). These words are not about perfection; they are about worthiness. They speak to a love that isn't dependent on polish or performance. They name the truth that can settle beneath your skin and rewrite every false story you've been handed.

When you see yourself through that lens—flawed but not broken, growing yet already enough—something inside begins to rest. You start showing up not to prove, but simply to be. You start speaking not to defend, but to declare.

So here is your invitation: step back into your own gaze with compassion. Let your reflection remind you, not critique you. Affirm the features you once questioned. Thank the body that has carried you through every battle. Forgive the younger you who didn't yet know how to fight for her light. Bless the woman you are still becoming—the one who is learning, unlearning, rising, and resting. The one defined not by rejection, but by truth.

You don't need the world to validate your beauty for it to be real. You only need to believe it enough to stop apologizing for it. Let this be your return—not to an ideal, but to yourself

Reclaiming my beauty was never just about how I looked—it was about how I *saw* myself. It was the moment I stopped apologizing for existing in full color, with all my depth, strength, and softness intact. That kind of acceptance doesn't end at the mirror; it moves into purpose. Because once you learn to see yourself through truth instead of distortion, you start to hear God's whisper more clearly. The same eyes that once searched for approval begin to look for assignment. The same reflection you once questioned becomes a reminder: you were created with intention.

And so, the next part of my journey wasn't about appearance at all—it was about alignment. About living the life my healing prepared me to walk in.

CHAPTER 21

Aligning with Your Purpose

I used to think purpose was something you discovered—like a prize hidden at the end of a perfectly followed roadmap. You go to school, get the job, check the boxes, and eventually it reveals itself: shining, obvious, divine. Over time I learned that purpose doesn't always arrive with fanfare. It often begins as a nudge—a persistent pull saying, *There's more to this life, and it has something to do with who you truly are.*

Purpose is less about reaching a destination and more about returning to yourself. It isn't tied only to career or titles. It shows up in the way you love people, how your presence softens a room, how your voice carries compassion, or how your story helps someone else feel seen. Purpose is woven into the fabric of how you live, love, and give—and it's often already there, waiting to be noticed.

There were seasons I overlooked my own purpose because it didn't look like someone else's calling. I saw other women moving boldly in their lane, their clarity sharp and their gifts defined, and I wondered if I was behind—if maybe I had missed my sign. Alignment, however, often requires unlearning. It means releasing borrowed dreams and expectations that never fit. Purpose blooms after you let go of what was never meant for you.

I began paying attention to what lit me up—not what appeared impressive, but what made me feel alive. Writing. Storytelling. Creating spaces where women could feel whole. Holding hands with the broken parts of people without needing to fix them. That wasn't merely passion—it was purpose speaking. And it didn't demand perfection from me; it simply asked that I be present.

Purpose rarely feels like grand celebrations. It feels like peace—like finally standing where you're meant to be, even when the world doesn't understand yet. It may look like raising a child in a way that heals wounds carried for generations. It may look like choosing joy after loss or praying over your business, your community, or your future self, trusting your words carry weight.

You don't need a platform to walk in purpose. Your kitchen table can be your altar. Your journal can be your pulpit. Your presence can be the most powerful sermon you'll ever preach. To align with purpose is to say yes to a life that fits your soul, not just your résumé. Purpose doesn't have to be profitable to be powerful.

Many women believe the lie that if something doesn't earn money or applause, it isn't worth much. Yet what about breaking generational chains in silence? What about loving deeply after heartbreak? What about breathing hope into places that once knew only pain? That is purpose. That is holy work.

Alignment happens when what you believe, what you value, and how you live and move in the same direction—when your inner world and outer actions echo one another. It may mean saying no to good things so you can say yes to the right ones. It means honoring your energy, protecting your peace, and declaring, *This is who I am now,* even when others remember an older version.

Alignment doesn't rush; it listens. Notice what makes you lose track of time. Pay attention to what breaks your heart and what mends it. Your purpose will always carry traces of your story—the pain, the joy, the lessons, the transformation. None of it is wasted. You've lived through too much not to be used for something beautiful. You don't have to chase purpose. Keep becoming, and let purpose find you.

There comes a moment when the noise of the world drowns out your spirit. That's when dissonance begins—not always in a dramatic way, but in the subtle ache saying, *This isn't it.* You smile, you show up, you do what's expected, yet your soul knows. It always knows.

Alignment is when that quiet ache becomes a call. I think of it like a tuning fork—the clear hum that rings when you've hit the note meant for you. For so long, I lived offbeat. I adjusted myself to rooms that didn't fit. I performed peace instead of living it. When I began asking, *What has God placed in me?* instead of *What do they want from me?*—everything shifted.

There's nothing louder than the silence of misalignment. You can be surrounded by praise and still feel empty. You can reach the "goal" and remain unfulfilled. That's when I realized that purpose isn't about doing good things; it's about doing the right things—the ones your spirit was designed to do.

Purpose rarely arrives with clarity. It begins as restlessness, a divine discomfort. You feel it in your chest, in your stomach, in the long exhale when you're finally alone. Something that once felt open now feels tight, and in that tension, God is speaking.

He doesn't always hand over instructions. Sometimes He offers a nudge—a gentle press on your heart. Sometimes it's a closed door, a missed opportunity, or a change you didn't ask for. Other times it's that persistent voice saying, *There's more.* We don't always recognize it as divine guidance. We call it anxiety, boredom, or restlessness. Yet what if it's God showing you that you've outgrown the room you're in—not because you're ungrateful, but because He's calling you higher?

I often return to this passage: *"A man's gift makes room for him and brings him before great men."* (Proverbs 18:16, NIV). Not effort. Not résumé. Not perfection—your gift. And gifts come with assignments. Purpose isn't about being seen; it's about serving, healing, creating, and making space for others to breathe. When you're aligned, purpose flows through you. You don't have to force it. You become the room, the light, the invitation.

Alignment is peace—not the absence of storms, but the stillness that remains even when the wind blows. I remember praying once, not for clarity but for peace: *God, if this is where I'm meant to be, let peace sit with me here. And if it's not, give me the courage to leave—even if I don't know where I'm going yet.* That prayer didn't make everything easy, but it made me honest. Honesty is the birthplace of alignment.

We often ask, *What is my purpose?* Maybe the better question is, *Where am I needed—just as I am, without shrinking? Where does my story unlock freedom in someone else? Where does my presence plant peace?* Purpose isn't a title; it's a truth you live. Living in alignment with it won't always look impressive. It may mean walking away from the crowd, starting over at thirty-seven, speaking softly when the world wants volume, or saying no when everyone expects yes.

When you find that fit, that rhythm, you know. Not because everything is perfect, but because you're no longer pretending. The most powerful testimony is often the one you didn't realize anyone was watching. When you live in alignment—with your values, your faith, and the truest parts of who you are—something shifts. You begin to heal not only for yourself but in a way that others can feel. Wholeness doesn't end with you—it ripples outward.

BLOOMING FORWARD

There's freedom in walking in step with your purpose—not because life is mastered, but because you've chosen to stop living for someone else's version of it. It's a quiet confidence that doesn't require constant explanation or applause. Alignment is less about chasing milestones and more about honoring the assignments already in your hands. It's showing up where you are, as you are, trusting that the way you love, speak, and serve carries its own divine weight.

Howard Thurman once said, "Don't ask yourself what the world needs. Ask yourself what makes you come alive, and go do that. Because what the world needs is people who have come alive." Those words stay with me because they speak to the heart of purpose—it isn't about bending yourself into shapes that win approval; it's about fully inhabiting the shape God has already given you. When you feel most alive, you often find you're most useful, because you're working from the wellspring of your own design.

Life can crowd out that aliveness. Expectations pile up, obligations multiply, and before long, you lose sight of what stirs your spirit. Alignment requires intentional reflection. Ask yourself: *Is this path nourishing me, or is it draining me? Does this choice honor the gifts I've been entrusted with, or am I simply doing what's expected?* These questions aren't meant to cause guilt; they're meant to bring you back to center.

"Many are the plans in a person's heart, but it is the Lord's purpose that prevails." (Proverbs 19:21, NIV). There's such relief in that truth. You can release the need to control every outcome and focus on faithfulness—showing up with the right heart even when you can't see the full picture. When you stop striving to orchestrate your own success, you leave room for God to direct your steps in ways you never could have planned.

Walking in alignment often means making hard choices. It might mean leaving spaces that no longer fit or setting boundaries others don't understand. It could mean stepping into opportunities that feel bigger than your confidence but smaller than your faith. Sometimes it means staying where you are, not out of fear, but because you know the assignment before you isn't finished yet.

The beauty of alignment is peace—even in the unknown. You may not have every detail worked out, yet you know you're moving in the right direction because the weight you once carried has lifted. There is room to breathe. You can give your best without losing yourself. You can pour into others without going empty because you're operating from overflow, not depletion.

As you bloom forward from here, reconnect with what makes you come alive. Notice the places, people, and practices that draw you closer to God's presence and your own truth. Let your days be guided not by the loudest demands but by the quiet, steady pull of your calling. And when doubts creep in—as they occasionally will—remember that you were created with intention. You are not a random arrangement of talents and traits. You are a deliberate work of art, placed here on purpose and for a purpose.

Keep saying yes to that truth. The rest will unfold exactly as it's meant to.

Living in alignment doesn't mean every space will celebrate your truth. Sometimes, walking in purpose exposes what no longer fits. The same light that reveals your path may also reveal people's projections—the ones who mistake your peace for pride or your boundaries for distance. Yet alignment teaches you not to shrink in those moments. You've worked too hard to lose yourself again. The next part of my journey was about learning to stand firm in who I'd become, even when being misunderstood felt uncomfortable.

CHAPTER 22

Graceful Disruption: The Strength of Staying True in Spaces that Misread You

They say pressure reveals character, but I've found it also reveals truth—about people, systems, and even about ourselves. The workplace became one of my greatest teachers. It showed me how environments can celebrate your skill and still test your spirit, how perception and reality can collide.

Working in those spaces taught me more than any promotion ever could. It revealed how success can magnify the unseen politics of belonging—how being visible in your excellence can also make you a mirror for other people's insecurities. That tension taught me to look deeper: not at who accepted me, but at how I carried myself when acceptance was uncertain.

Maybe you've felt that too—the quiet tension that fills a room before you've even spoken. You're competent, steady, calm. You do your work with grace, but your calm somehow feels like a threat to those who thrive on control or comparison.

I've never been the loudest voice in the room. My leadership doesn't rise through volume or force. I don't respond to every slight, direct or indirect, or raise my voice just to prove I have one. Yet that calm, that refusal to meet fire with fire, often unsettled people even more—especially women who looked like me.

That was the part I didn't expect. Resistance from certain corners, yes—but tension from those I assumed would understand—the women who shared my identity—cut differently. Instead of solidarity, I sometimes encountered competition, suspicion, or misplaced aggression. It's a dynamic we rarely name aloud, but it exists. When you are poised, professional, and self-possessed, it can be read as pretense. When you carry quiet confidence, it can be mistaken for arrogance. When you hold your peace and work with steady excellence, it can stir insecurities you didn't create but are suddenly asked to soothe.

If you choose not to play into that cycle—if you don't clap back, dim your light, or apologize for your calm—the tension grows. That's when the smear campaign begins—not always in loud accusations, but in whispers and quiet omissions. Your name disappears from the email chain; your work gets overlooked in the meeting. It's rarely blatant, but consistent enough to chip away at belonging.

Those moments leave an imprint. They remind you that even subtle exclusion can echo loudly when all you're trying to do is show up and do your work with grace.

Dislike is not the issue. Not everyone will connect, and that's human. Personalities clash. Some people simply won't be your cup of tea, and that's okay. The harm begins when discomfort turns into attempts to isolate, with the hope of pushing you out. That's where trust fractures. After moments of misplaced trust—when kindness was mistaken for weakness—it became harder to know who was safe. My trust issues didn't begin at work, but the workplace magnified them.

If you've ever been there—wondering who's genuine and who's performing kindness—you understand the emotional math it takes to stay both open and wise. You spend energy deciding when to speak and when to stay silent, when to engage and when to protect your peace. It's exhausting at times, but discernment, I've learned, doesn't mean walking around guarded; it means moving with intention.

These experiences taught me the difference between peace and passivity. I don't have to defend every misperception or correct every narrative. I've learned to lead with discernment, not suspicion—to observe, protect my peace, and hold space for myself even when others try to minimize it.

And here's the truth that steadied me: not every distance is a betrayal; sometimes it's simply difference. Everyone isn't meant to connect, and that's okay. Harmony isn't forced—it's chosen through mutual respect.

Because I've learned: a smile doesn't always mean loyalty. Shared identity doesn't always mean shared integrity. And just because your name is mentioned in a room doesn't mean you need to walk into it.

Let them talk. Let them assume. You can still do your work—with grace, with strength, and without apology. Staying true to yourself doesn't require explanation; it requires alignment. Integrity has a confidence that doesn't need an audience.

The irony is that the very word I once used to empower others—qualify—was later used against me. For years, I encouraged women to qualify people before granting them access to their emotional sanctuaries. Smiles and laughter don't automatically make someone safe. Trust must be earned. But when I began applying that same wisdom to protect my own peace, others twisted it into something else: *She's not qualified.*

Never mind the years of preparation, the work ethic, the integrity, or the consistency. When people only see the polished calm, they assume you haven't earned your place—or worse, that you shouldn't have it at all. That's the tax of composure: being misread because you don't mirror chaos.

This is the disruption of being a Black woman who refuses to play the expected role. You stop apologizing for your light, and suddenly your presence feels too bright for some rooms. You speak with calm conviction instead of noise, and people mistake it for distance. You lead with discernment instead of drama, and it gets labeled as detachment. You choose integrity over performance, and they call it cold.

But clarity has its own warmth. The peace that comes from knowing who you are and what you will no longer tolerate carries its own steady fire.

If you've felt that tension, you're not alone. Many of us have walked into rooms where our very presence disrupted unspoken rules—where confidence was mistaken for competition and grace for distance. But you were never meant to pretend to fit just to be accepted.

The truth is simpler: you're intentional. You know your worth and no longer confuse access with entitlement. That clarity is a form of freedom. When you live from it, your peace becomes visible—even in silence. You no longer chase approval; you embody alignment.

So if qualifying people or guarding your peace makes others uncomfortable, let it. You don't owe anyone your energy, your vulnerability, or your truth. You owe it to yourself to move through this world with wisdom, integrity, and grace.

As you do, you'll find that the right people—those who honor your peace and see your light as strength—will meet you where you are. They won't compete with your calm; they'll feel at home in it.

What most people never see are the years it took to build that peace—the inner battles you fought just to feel safe in rooms you had already earned entry into, the boundaries you shaped so you could stand tall without dimming your light. Being qualified isn't about titles or tenure; it's about wisdom, integrity, and courage. It's knowing your value even when others try to negotiate it down to something more comfortable for them.

And this journey isn't just about climbing ladders or proving skill; it's about protecting your soul while you rise. It's about refusing to let someone else's insecurities define your reflection. It's about continuing to grow with grace, even when grace is withheld from you.

There's a cost to moving differently. When you don't gossip, overshare, or trade vulnerability for validation, people don't know how to read you. So they create stories of their own—*She thinks she's better. She's not a team player. She's cold.* But discernment isn't arrogance. Silence isn't weakness. Guarding your peace isn't isolation—it's wisdom in motion.

Over time, I stopped trying to understand the why. Not every slight needs decoding. I began focusing instead on the women who choose connection over competition—the ones who clap for you when no one's watching. They remind me that collaboration is power, not threat. Those are the circles that restore faith, where authenticity is celebrated and everyone's light is safe to shine.

I also found something deeper in those moments of genuine connection—proof that grace exists even in complex spaces. There were colleagues who saw me clearly, who valued collaboration over comparison. We worked side by side, lifting each other's ideas higher instead of guarding them. Those exchanges reminded me that integrity still has allies, that goodness still thrives quietly in corners of the workplace where ego doesn't lead.

The beauty of those relationships was their honesty. They didn't demand perfection, only respect. We learned from one another's strengths, covered each other's blind spots, and practiced grace in real time. That kind of connection doesn't erase the challenges, but it makes them bearable. It reminds you that light recognizes light, even in the most competitive environments.

Those friendships became anchors—reminders that every workplace holds both challenge and grace. For every room that misread me, there was another where I felt seen. For every misunderstanding, there was a moment of genuine collaboration that restored faith in what's possible when we lead with empathy, not ego.

Those moments taught me that "graceful disruption" isn't only about standing firm when misunderstood—it's also about building bridges where understanding is possible. It's knowing when to guard your peace and when to open your hand to community. Both can coexist—and both are necessary.

Even then, don't move from bitterness. I've wanted to match energy, but that would make me no different. Knowing that truth has saved me from words I couldn't take back and battles that would have drained me. Let your work speak. Let your integrity echo. That becomes its own steady resistance—quiet to some but freeing to you.

Being calm, thoughtful, and intentional is often misread. But those who know the storms you've survived understand that your strength doesn't need to be loud to be real. Your calm is not emptiness—it's evidence of healing. The resilience you carry has been earned through silence, prayer, and choosing not to be hardened by what tried to break you.

Guard the softest parts of yourself—not out of fear, but out of wisdom. Not everyone earns a seat at your table, and that's not arrogance; it's discernment. Protect the sacred spaces of your growth from those who only know how to consume it. Access to your energy, your peace, and your story is a privilege, not a guarantee. Reserve it for those who show up with consistency, truth, and care.

This season of life may be teaching you to stand taller, not harder—to lead with quiet strength and grounded confidence. To protect your peace as though it were the crown jewel of your legacy. To keep showing up fully yourself, even when others misunderstand your light. Because you don't have to fold to belong.

It takes courage to remain yourself in spaces that ask you to be anything else. To walk into rooms where your calm is questioned, your strength misread, and your presence feels disruptive—and still choose to stand tall. That isn't weakness; that's wisdom forged through fire.

Everyone's path toward peace looks different. Some need to speak loudly to feel seen; others find strength in stillness. Not everyone will meet you where you are, and that's all right. We're all learning how to lead ourselves back to calm.

Peace, I've learned, isn't a preference. It's a boundary, a decision, and a way of life. True peace doesn't need validation or translation; it protects what's sacred within you. The world may not always understand a woman who leads with grace instead of ego, but that's not your concern. You weren't created to be deciphered by those still at war with themselves.

My heart carries deep respect for all women, but I have a special admiration for women of color—for our brilliance, creativity, and resilience. We carry so much and still manage to create beauty from burden. Though we are often the least protected, we continue to show up, lead, nurture, and build space for others. That's why it can be disheartening when comparison creeps in and competition replaces connection. Somewhere along the way, we were convinced that only one of us could shine at a time. But that was never true. Our light multiplies. Our power expands when we pour into one another. The more we honor each other's journeys, the freer we all become.

Graceful disruption begins here—with refusing to mirror the world's scarcity mindset and choosing community over competition. It's reclaiming the truth that we rise stronger together. This is reclaiming season: a time to release the illusion of perfection, to speak truth with compassion, and to take up space without apology.

When you walk into rooms that weren't designed for your light, remember: you are not there to prove you belong. You are there to embody peace, purpose, and presence. And if those rooms still misread you, build new ones—spaces where authenticity, excellence, and empathy coexist. Your calm is not complacency; it's confidence. Your discernment is not detachment; it's depth. You were never meant to fit inside someone else's smallness.

BLOOMING FORWARD

There comes a moment when you realize peace is more than preference—it's protection. You stop rushing to explain yourself and start moving in rhythm with what guards your growth. The world may still misinterpret your calm, but you weren't called to perform for understanding; you were called to live in truth.

Discernment isn't coldness—it's clarity. It teaches you to choose who earns access to your presence and who no longer does. Guarding your peace isn't selfish; it's stewardship. You learn that you don't have to quiet your voice to belong or dim your light to make others comfortable. But balance also means leaving room for grace—for the people who do see you, who meet you with respect, and who hold space for your growth without demanding you shrink.

The truth is, every space holds both challenge and possibility. When you meet others who lead with humility, collaboration, and care, you're reminded that goodness still thrives quietly—even in places where competition used to be the loudest voice. Those connections heal something deeper. They remind you that leadership doesn't always look like commanding a room; sometimes it's two people exchanging trust, or a team moving as one without ego at the center.

Toni Morrison once wrote, "If you want to fly, you have to give up the things that weigh you down." Sometimes those weights are not people but the habits that keep us guarded—the over-explaining, the proving, the pretending to be unaffected.

We release them not to become harder, but freer. When you walk in truth, you stop managing perception and start trusting your reflection.

You're not too much, fragile, or detached—you're focused. You're aligned. Living this way teaches you that real peace doesn't isolate; it invites what's genuine to draw near. You begin to notice the people who honor your boundaries as easily as they celebrate your brilliance. Those are your anchors. Those are your allies.

And when pressure builds—when others mistake your confidence for arrogance or your restraint for indifference—come back to what centers you:
"Let the peace of Christ rule in your hearts, since as members of one body you were called to peace. And be thankful." (Colossians 3:15, NIV)

That kind of peace doesn't hush the world; it steadies you within it. It reminds you that your worth isn't negotiable, your presence isn't accidental, and your light was never meant to be filtered through someone else's fear. So keep showing up. Keep leading with grace. Keep building bridges where understanding is possible, and when necessary, stand firm in your truth. Your light isn't a threat—it's an invitation. And those who are meant for your peace will never feel burned by it.

CHAPTER 23

Cultivating Resilience

Resilience. For much of my life, that word felt like a shield I didn't ask to wear—heavy, expected, yet necessary. People said it as if it were a compliment: "You're so strong," "You always bounce back," "I don't know how you do it." I smiled politely while wondering, Do I even have a choice? I once thought survival and resilience were the same. But survival is what carries you through; resilience is what helps you become because of it.

I didn't realize I was shaping resilience as I moved through my own storms. What once felt like survival began to feel too small. I no longer wanted to "get through." I wanted to live through it—to grow, to learn, to rise differently. And that's when I understood: resilience isn't about bouncing back to who you were. It's about rising as someone wiser, steadier, and more whole. That realization changed how I saw everything. Growth wasn't only about endurance anymore; it was about allowing myself to evolve in gentler ways. True strength, I learned, wasn't found in doing it all alone but in opening myself to receive support—the very thing I once resisted.

Asking for help once felt complicated. Too often, help was used as leverage or thrown back in my face. So I learned to depend on myself, leaving little room to crumble. My unspoken rule was simple: cry if you must, then move forward. That mindset helped me endure, but it also made isolation look like strength.

I used to wonder why some people seem to carry resilience so naturally while others struggle to find their footing. Over time, I've realized it isn't about who's stronger—it's about how we've been shaped. Some learned resilience in the safety of support; others built it in the dark, piecing together strength from what little they had. For some, it's a soft endurance that hums beneath the surface; for others, it's a roar that says, "I'm still here." Both are sacred. Both are strength. What looks effortless on the outside often carries a private cost. The truth is, no one emerges from struggle unchanged—we just learn to wear our survival differently.

Over time, I came to understand another kind of resilience—steady, lived, and soul-deep. Not the kind that looks solid in public but cracks in private. The kind that says, *I'm still standing,* without needing to announce it. True resilience isn't about silence or suppression; it's about courage. It's standing in the same space that once tested you and realizing you're no longer the same. It's admitting you're not okay while trusting you won't stay there. It's learning that sometimes strength looks like rest.

Resilience can be both cultivated and inherited. It grows in small, ordinary moments no one applauds—when you speak instead of staying silent, when you open your heart again after betrayal, when you choose gentleness in a world that rewards hardness. It isn't formed in the absence of fire but within it—not because the flames are fair, but because you refuse to be defined by them.

I've always known resilience lived in me, though for years I wondered why it seemed to show up more naturally for some and less for others. What I've learned is that resilience isn't about being untouched by pain—it's about how you rise from it. It doesn't always look the same. For some, it's loud and visible; for others, it's quiet and steady. Either way, it lives within us all, waiting for the right moment to emerge.

At this point in my life, resilience feels less like recovery and more like rhythm. It's not something I reach for in crisis; it's the steadiness that carries me between the highs and lows. I no longer measure strength by what I survive, but by how I stay centered when nothing needs surviving.

What we don't always admit is that resilience isn't effortless. Even steady strength can ache at times. It asks something of you—to stay open when closing off would be easier, to trust the process when progress feels invisible. Yet that's where its quiet beauty lives: not in perfection, but in presence. There will be days when tears come easily, when hope feels thin. But even then, grace holds you steady. Strength doesn't mean you never bend—it means you know how to return to center.

Breaking doesn't mean you've failed. Crying doesn't mean you've lost strength. Resting doesn't mean you've quit. Resilience never demands perfection—it simply asks you to remain present. I used to think unraveling meant I was falling apart, but I've learned it can also mean renewal beginning. Strength isn't proven in how tightly you hold things together; it's revealed in your willingness to release what no longer serves you and trust what's being rebuilt.

And rebuild I did—not overnight, and not without scar tissue. Resilience, I've learned, is less about bouncing back and more about blooming forward. It's the art of rebuilding with intention, of choosing peace even when pain still lingers. You tend to what remains, water what's left, and trust that new life will rise from what was broken. Healing often happens underground—quiet, unseen, but deeply transformative. One day you look back and realize: you didn't just survive—you grew.

And still standing is a testimony. Not loud or performative, but steady and true. We don't always give ourselves credit for what it takes to keep showing up—not out of obligation, but out of love for life itself. Real strength doesn't boast; it breathes. It speaks through your perseverance; through the way you keep choosing hope when no one's watching.

Resilience isn't about constant motion; it's about consistent becoming. It's waking up on the days that feel heavy and still deciding to believe in the possibility of light. It's forgiving yourself for how long it takes to heal. It's honoring your humanity, not just your endurance.

And resilience doesn't thrive in isolation—it deepens in connection. We need safe places to exhale, people who remind us of our worth, and rhythms that help us rest. Stillness is not a pause from growth; it's a vital part of it. Peace has a way of replanting what pain tried to uproot.

You are not strong because you suffered well; you are strong because you allowed yourself to rise well. Because you learned to keep becoming. Because you let grace lead the way. Wholeness isn't hardness—it's softness fortified by wisdom. The most powerful resilience still chooses tenderness.

So when the world says to toughen up, remember: resilience isn't about being unbreakable. It's about being beautifully rebuilt. Every scar becomes a signature of survival, every breath a reminder that grace still carries you

Now, with the strength you've cultivated and the gentleness you've reclaimed, you are ready to rise—not only as a survivor, but as someone deeply, divinely whole.

BLOOMING FORWARD

Resilience isn't something you chase; it's something you cultivate. It grows quietly through presence, grace, and a willingness to begin again. It doesn't demand that you stay strong every moment—it asks that you stay true. When you choose gentleness over self-judgment, you are practicing resilience. When you rest without guilt, you are strengthening what sustains you.

True resilience honors your limits as much as your potential. It makes space for grief without surrendering hope. It's not about proving how much you can handle, but learning how to nurture what helps you heal. Sometimes that looks like pausing. Sometimes it looks like choosing joy even when life feels uncertain. Always, it looks like faith in motion.

Audre Lorde once wrote, "When I dare to be powerful—to use my strength in the service of my vision—it becomes less and less important whether I am afraid." That is resilience in its purest form—the courage to keep showing up for your own life, even when fear still lingers at the edges.

And when your heart feels unsteady, remember: "My flesh and my heart may fail, but God is the strength of my heart and my portion forever" (Psalm 73:26, NIV). That strength isn't earned by striving; it's received through surrender. It's the peace that comes when you stop fighting your story and begin to trust its purpose.

You don't have to bloom on command. You don't have to be unshakable. Staying open to growth, to hope, and to the quiet unfolding of who you're becoming—that's more than enough.

CHAPTER 24

Inspiring Others Through Your Journey

F inding peace within isn't about having it all together. It isn't smiling through pain or pretending the hard things never happened. It begins when you stop running from your story and embrace every part of it—the broken pieces, the healed places, and the ones still unfolding. I'd lived with the thought that becoming whole meant fixing everything—silencing every doubt, mending every wound, and tying my life in a neat bow before I could claim my worth. But peace within isn't flawlessness; it's learning to live in harmony with your becoming.

To live fully is to honor who you were, love who you are, and make space for who you're still becoming. It's standing in the full truth of your story—joy and grief, triumph and failure—and saying, *This is mine.* Pain doesn't get to define you or write the ending. Even when the ache resurfaces in peaceful seasons or laughter's midst, peace within acknowledges pain but doesn't let it lead. Becoming doesn't erase struggle; it teaches you how to live beyond it—with grace as your quiet guide.

Living at peace with yourself also means embracing your humanity—soft and strong, healed and healing, grounded and growing. It's the brave choice to stop performing strength and allow yourself to simply be. To cry when you need to. To laugh without apology. To take up space without explanation. Belonging isn't earned, and value isn't proven. You are worthy because you're here—because your existence carries meaning before you ever prove a thing.

That truth takes time to settle, especially in a world that trains us to hustle for approval. Peace within interrupts that pattern. Productivity doesn't equal worth, and popularity doesn't guarantee love. You don't have to be everything to everyone to be enough for yourself. This is the gentle reclamation of value—the remembering that true strength comes from stillness, not striving.

While writing this book, I met countless women who shared glimpses of their own journeys. Many, like me, had spent years believing they had to prove their worth before they could finally exhale. Listening to them reminded me that none of us walk this path alone. The details may differ, but the ache is familiar—the desire to be seen, to feel safe, to belong without having to perform for it.

Peace within isn't about palatability; it's about truth. It's unlearning the belief that authenticity must be traded for acceptance. It's calling back every fragment you gave away trying to be loved and saying clearly, *I am not too much. I am not broken. I am enough, even as I grow.* Calling yourself back—the voice you hushed, the joy you muted—creates freedom that doesn't rely on anyone else's permission to exist.

We live in a world that rewards polish and confuses vulnerability with weakness. It celebrates what appears reflective but avoids what's real—the rawness, the questions, the parts that don't tie up neatly. True reflection isn't tidy. It's honest. It's sometimes uncomfortable, always revealing. Yet we've been conditioned to make our healing digestible, to share only what feels safe for others to witness. But the unpolished moments—the trembling truth-telling, the courage to show up unsure—carry the most light.

There's power in releasing the idea that worth is measured by productivity or approval. When you stop chasing validation, new questions begin to guide your life:

What moments make me feel most at home in my body, most connected to peace within myself?

Do my choices reflect what I value in how I live, love, and lead?

Peace within reminds you that you're already complete—right here, as you are. Not because everything is resolved, but because your presence holds purpose. Through grace, you learn to exhale where you once held your breath. Your steps grow lighter. Compassion replaces critique. You begin walking away from the roles that kept you small and rewriting the rules that once defined your survival. Soft yet powerful. Grounded yet open. Healing and becoming.

The beauty of becoming is that it never stays contained. As you grow gentler with yourself, others feel it. They notice it in how you listen, how you move through rooms, how you no longer chase belonging but create it. Your becoming becomes a mirror—a reflection that healing is possible.

And in this becoming, you begin to inspire.

You don't need a stage or an audience. Your life speaks when you live with hope, courage, and grace. You give others permission to be real, to heal, to tell the truth. Transformation becomes visible—not because life grew easy, but because you stopped hiding and started showing up as your full self.

A story doesn't have to be complete to be meaningful. People don't connect to perfection; they connect to honesty and resilience. They recognize your decision to keep showing up while life is still unfolding—in how you handle heartbreak, the compassion you choose over judgment, and the steadiness in your presence. Those are the imprints that linger.

Your journey becomes your legacy. What matters most is your willingness to be seen—not for applause, but for truth. Every time you show up as yourself, you clear space for someone else to do the same.

As we learn to honor our stories, we naturally extend that grace to others. Sharing can be simple—mentoring someone walking a familiar path, writing a short reflection, encouraging a friend who feels stuck, or simply listening without judgment. Sometimes the most powerful ministry is quiet presence. Small connections create lasting ripples.

Like the women who shared their journeys with me. Or the friend who forgave herself after years of carrying blame. These moments, quiet as they are, ripple outward. Listening also heals. When you sit with someone's truth and hold it gently, you become part of their restoration and deepen your own. That is the reciprocity of growth—when you heal, others breathe easier near you. When you live honestly, others find courage to face their truth. When you stop hiding, your light reaches those still in shadow.

Your story *is* your legacy. Every time you choose authenticity over approval, tenderness over pretense, faith over fear, you model something powerful. You remind the world that peace is possible—imperfect, often gentle, yet deeply transformative. Speak your truth. Share your light. Let your becoming be a lighthouse—open-handed, grace-filled, led by love. As you rise—heart open, story whole, spirit anchored—remember becoming isn't about where you've been, but what you're building now. It's the legacy you're shaping through every honest breath, every brave yes, and every act of grace toward yourself and others.

BLOOMING FORWARD

Relief comes when you realize perfection was never required to make an impact. Many of us were taught to arrive polished before offering anything of value. Yet a life speaks—even in its unfinished places. The courage to be real, to keep becoming, to show compassion to yourself—that's what inspires. Strength doesn't need performance, and softness doesn't need disguise. No platform is required. When truth is honored, ripples follow. Integrity in small moments—kind words, an owned story, lived values—plants seeds that matter.

Morgan Harper Nichols reminds us, *"Tell the story of the mountain you climbed. Your words could become a page in someone else's survival guide."* Often it isn't advice that saves—it's example. The grace in your presence, the way you kept going, the space you created for others to breathe. That is legacy. Not mastery, but honesty. Not polish, but process. It says, *I've walked through things—and I'm still here.*

Lead with presence. Extend to others the same grace you're still learning to give yourself. When words come—on paper, in conversation, through action—let them be an offering, a bridge, a steady light that says, *Me too. You're not alone.* Take your time.

The full impact may never be visible. Someone sees you live with peace and realizes it's possible. Another hears your laughter and remembers joy. Someone else witnesses your gentleness and decides to lay down their armor. Healing moves from heart to heart, story to story—often unseen, always felt.

"Being confident of this," Philippians 1:6 (NIV) promises, *"that he who began a good work in you will carry it on to completion."*
There's no need to rush the outcome. Keep becoming. Live open-handed, with a heart rooted in grace.

Your life is the light. That is enough.

CHAPTER 25
Pen, Purpose, and Legacy

If you had asked little Victoria who she wanted to be, you would've needed a full notebook. One moment I was choreographing routines, baby oil slicked through my hair to nail the Michael Jackson curl. The next, I was accepting imaginary awards in a glittery dress, channeling Diana Ross. Some days I argued cases in my mind's courtroom; other days I lived among library stacks; most days I wrote stories only I could see.

I dreamed wide and loud—without apology. Dreaming was survival. It gave me somewhere to go when life felt heavy. It tethered me to something larger than hurt. Not fantasy, but fuel.

Books became my escape and my education. Reading soon deepened into writing—journals, poems, scraps of scenes. Over time, desire sharpened: I wanted to publish. Not just once, but again and again, under my own imprint.

Inspired by years in the Carolinas, I formed a press and began what I thought would be my debut novel, *Say Yes*. For the first time, I was breathing life into a childhood dream.

Then came grief—wave after wave. My stepdad, grandmother, a dear friend and mentor, and then my father passed. Loss felt relentless. I could not finish grieving one before the next arrived. Added to this was the pressure of a high-stress career, caregiving, betrayals from people I called friends, and health challenges that left me depleted. I went into defense mode by building walls, burying disappointment. And I stayed there a long time.

Grief had stripped me bare, but it also carved space for something new to root. Beneath the weight of loss, I began to see how purpose had been quietly waiting—not to replace the pain, but to transform it. Some of those walls still stand. Bricks are coming down slowly. Healing isn't a race; it honors layers and timing.

Through every season, I've learned that becoming invites many versions of you to emerge. Each one has its own lessons, its own language, its own light. Some seasons require you to let go of habits that once felt like protection. Others ask you to release identities that no longer fit who you're becoming. Every version of me has taught something essential—how to listen deeper, how to rest easier, how to lead from authenticity instead of survival. Shedding isn't loss; it's refinement. You outgrow what once anchored you so you can expand into new strength. Every evolution is both an ending and an invitation to live more truthfully.

About six years ago, something shifted. I reviewed every corner of my life—seen and hidden—and listed the changes I needed. Some came quickly; others required planning, prayer, and patience. I began. A major step was pulling out the drafts I had tucked away: outlines, character sketches, world notes. As I sifted through them, I sensed *Bella's Blues* should lead. Even then, something felt missing, as if I were skipping a foundation. Then it landed: my story needed to come first—not just the fiction, but the journey of the woman behind the storyteller—the one who fought for her own voice before she ever shared it with the world.

During that same season, an unexpected opportunity opened a door for me to share more of my story beyond my comfort zone. It reminded me that sometimes, healing begins the moment you stop hiding. Around the same time, I was named a Top 50 Author Allstars for 2024–2025 and received the Presidential Lifetime Achievement Award. Both honors mattered; the latter carried an unspoken weight. *Lifetime.* Holding it, I saw a reel of moments—trials and triumphs stitched together. Sleepless nights. Sacrifices. Advocacy, mentorship, service. I realized I hadn't just survived. I kept showing up.

Recognition didn't feel like arrival—it felt like confirmation. Proof that faith, persistence, and grace had done their quiet work. Each milestone reminded me that what begins in private obedience can one day ripple into public purpose. Those opportunities did what they were meant to do. They readied me to step into my next chapter—not simply as a writer or publisher, but as a woman choosing to bloom. Not in spite of what I walked through, but because of it.

My Grandma Rosie would say, "Somebody hoped me along the way." That is what I want this book to be: a source of hope. For the girl fighting to believe her story matters. The woman rediscovering herself after years behind a role. Or the heart healing in layers and still choosing to show up.

I don't have all the answers, nor am I writing from the mindset of arrival. I'm writing from a truth I trust: power lives in owning your story. Freedom lives in speaking it. Healing lives in realizing every curve, turn, and delay still led you here—right on time.

Maybe that's the beauty—growth isn't a finish line. It's a life. With each dream resurrected, each story reclaimed, each time you show up softer and stronger, you write another echo of your living. Little Victoria still lives in me—wide-eyed, curious, bold. She isn't just dreaming now. She's building. And with every word I write, I honor her. The becoming never ends—it keeps writing itself through every story you dare to tell.

BLOOMING FORWARD

Meaning often emerges when you circle back to the beginning—not to relive the past, but to reclaim the parts of yourself that never stopped dreaming. Before, small hands held more than they should.

Little you is not a memory to mourn. She's a spark that never went out, the first to imagine more. She doesn't need perfection; she needs truth. Shape a life that honors her resilience, her hope, her voice. You are not starting from scratch; you are carrying forward an inheritance of faith and light that began the moment she believed more was possible.

When healing feels slow and grief and hope take turns at your side, remember: this life proves she made it. She mattered—and still does.

Sue Monk Kidd once wrote, "The soul often knows what to do to heal itself. The challenge is to silence the mind." Turn down the noise of expectation and doubt so the steady truth you've carried all along can rise again: you are evolving into who you were always meant to be.

Even here, the unfolding continues—returning to the parts of you that waited to be heard, showing up in fullness, because beauty is found in the process. Pause without guilt. Rest without shame. Love without condition. Rise with intention.

Most of all, you've learned your voice—gentle or bold, unsteady or sure—is a worthy instrument of truth. No platform or title is required. Your life and presence—your unfolding—are your legacy. It shows in how you nurture what once broke you, how you hold space for your own softness, and how you step forward with purpose, grace, and dignity.

And when doubt creeps in, remember the promise of Psalm 138:8 (NIV): "The Lord will fulfill his purpose for me; your steadfast love, O Lord, endures forever." You haven't missed your moment. You aren't behind. You are exactly where you need to be.

Becoming doesn't end at a destination. It continues every time you honor truth, reclaim dreams, and live out loud in the light of everything you've survived. Keep saying yes to the life you were made for.

CONCLUSION

The Becoming Never Ends: Living the Transformation

This journey was never about perfection, or about fixing everything, or becoming someone brand new. It was about returning—to yourself. Beneath the noise, the armor, the expectations, the survival. It has always been about reclaiming the parts of you that were buried under the weight of being everything for everyone else—the soft, strong, enduring parts that have always been yours.

The journey to you is not a destination but a continual unfolding—a gentle remembering that your worth was never in question. You were never lost, only hidden. And now, you are rising.

With sparks of hope lighting the way, you have walked through shadows. You've stood in storms with courage trembling in your chest yet refusing to let go. Even when unseen battles raged, you spoke grace over yourself. You've looked in the mirror and, maybe for the first time, seen not the version you had to be—but who you truly are.

The truth about transformation is that it isn't linear. It doesn't always roar in triumph. Sometimes it looks like sitting still and choosing not to abandon yourself. In other moments, it's soft and subtle—found in the decision to try again, or the breath you take when fear tells you that you can't and you move forward anyway. It's the glimmer of hope in the darkness, the courage to take one step, the grace to be gentle with yourself along the way.

At the Mint Museum in Charlotte, I often paused to admire a sculpture called *Flutter* by Eva Hild. It reminded me of womanhood—of the many curves and bends that shape who we are, and how we hold so much inside us, sometimes all at once. The piece carried undeniable presence. Just like us. Just like this journey. *Flutter* felt like a reflection of growth—softness, complexity, resilience—and it reminded me that even in stillness, we are in motion.

You've lived the themes of this book in real time—hope, courage, and grace. Now you carry them in your bones, in your choices, in the way you show up to your life. And still, the unfolding continues. There will be new versions of you that emerge—each one asking you to shed what no longer fits, to stretch into what's next, to trust that change doesn't erase who you've been; it expands her.

There will be days when you forget who you are—days when your past feels louder than your progress. But now, you have tools. You have truth. You have a map drawn from everything you've survived. You know the way back home—to yourself.

Hope doesn't have to shout. It can be a steady flame in the middle of the storm, a light that keeps burning even when the night is long. Courage isn't always a battle cry; sometimes it's simply putting one foot in front of the other. Grace is the thread that weaves it all together, reminding you that even your missteps are part of the masterpiece.

Transformation never stops with you—it ripples outward, shaping families, friendships, and futures. Living your truth empowers others to do the same. Your story matters. Your healing matters. The sound of your becoming lights the path for someone who thought she was alone.

So let this be a reminder: the journey you're on is valid. Softness is strength. Life, as it is, is worthy of celebration—not because it's perfect, but because it's real.

Keep going. Keep blooming. Keep showing up for every version of who you're becoming.

Because becoming continues in every breath you take... and your next chapter is already waiting for you to step inside.

BONUS CONTENT

The Journey to You Self-Inventory: A Reflection for the Road Ahead

This isn't a checklist to measure progress. It's a pause to listen to yourself — to take honest inventory of what feels aligned, what's shifting, and what still asks for your attention. You've journeyed through pages of truth, healing, and courage. Now, this space belongs to you. It's not about who the world expects you to be, but who you are when no one else is watching.

Take your time. Sit with each question. Be unfiltered, bold, and compassionate. When you're done, read your words not to analyze but to understand. Notice what repeats, what resists, and what feels ready to grow roots. This is about awareness, not arrival — about building a rhythm of honesty with yourself.

Reflecting on Your Past

Begin by looking back — not to stay there, but to understand what shaped you and how those experiences still live in your choices today.

1.   Where do you feel most like yourself, and how can you bring more of that energy into your daily life?

2.   When was the last time you felt fully at peace in your own skin? What was present, and what was missing?

3.   What do you want to feel more of in this next season, and what do you need to release to make room for it?

4.   What dream have you kept on the back burner that may be asking for your attention again?

5.   What forms of beauty, power, or truth have you been hiding, and what would it look like to let them be seen?

6.   What parts of yourself have you recently reclaimed that you didn't realize had been hidden or silenced?

Embracing Your Present

Now, turn to where you stand. Awareness begins here —
in how you tend to yourself, protect your peace, and live your
truth each day.

7.   In what ways have you neglected yourself —
emotionally, spiritually, or creatively — and what would care
look like now?

8.   What have you been taught to fear that you now feel
ready to face?

9.   When was the last time you surprised yourself with
your own strength, tenderness, or wisdom?

10. What version of you are you outgrowing, and what new
way of being are you beginning to embody?

11. What identities, titles, or roles no longer fit the person
you're becoming?

12. Where in your life are you showing up from obligation instead of alignment?

13. Whose voice still echoes in your decisions, and does it deserve to remain there?

14. How have your roots, culture, or community shaped how you see yourself — and how you love?

Envisioning Your Future

Finally, look forward. This is about movement — the quiet courage to live what you've learned and create a life that reflects it.

15. What parts of your story have you never spoken aloud, and what would it mean to give them voice now?

16. If you stripped away titles, roles, and responsibilities, who would remain? What does she need to hear today?

17. What does emotional safety look like for you now, and how can you protect it with kindness and clarity?

18. What habits, patterns, or stories are you ready to stop rehearsing, and what vision of your next chapter feels alive and possible?

19. What would it look like to live with more intention—less reacting, more creating—and where could you begin that shift today?

20. How do you want to be remembered—not by what you achieved, but by how you made others feel and how fully you lived your truth?

Action & Integration

This inventory is a mirror, not a mandate. Let what surfaced guide your next small, faithful steps. Maybe that means journaling, praying, resting, setting a boundary, or sharing one truth aloud for the first time. Choose one action that feels gentle but real.

You don't have to rush to make meaning from your answers. Growth is revealed in awareness and practice, not perfection. Keep this inventory nearby. Revisit it whenever you feel disconnected. Let it remind you of the woman you are becoming — and the one you have always been.

You've done the sacred work of looking within—of slowing down long enough to listen. What comes next doesn't have to be perfect; it only needs to be honest. Let what you've uncovered guide how you show up in the world: with compassion, courage, and peace. Keep choosing awareness over urgency, truth over performance, and grace over guilt. Every time you return to yourself, you honor the life you've been given and the woman you are still becoming.

"My life is mine. And it is unfolding at the pace it's meant to."
— **Tracee Ellis Ross**

ACKNOWLEDGEMENTS

To my Heavenly Father — where would I be without Your grace? Through every season of my life—through the heartbreaks, the detours, the losses I didn't think I could survive—You carried me through. This book is my testimony, a reflection of Your mercy and the strength You planted inside me long before I ever knew how deeply I'd need it. I know without a shadow of a doubt it is because of you that I have made it thus far.

To my mother—my heart—Ms. Sewell. Our journey hasn't been easy, but it's been ours. Through every high and every valley, through the distance and the closeness, one thing has never changed: the love we carry for one another. You taught me resilience not through words, but through how you've lived. You've endured, sacrificed, and yet you still show up for others with compassion. That kind of strength doesn't go unnoticed. I love you more than these words can hold.

To the women who stepped into my life like answered prayers—Ms. Marshall and Mrs. Averhart. You didn't just encourage me professionally. You embraced me personally, like a daughter. I know God aligned our paths because He knew

I needed to feel seen, nurtured, and supported in ways that mirrored a mother's love. Thank you for being my bonus moms—for loving me, guiding me, and reminding me that I am never alone.

To Mr. Averhart—thank you for being a quiet strength, a steady example of what it means to love well and show up with integrity. Watching the way you love your wife, witnessing that tenderness and partnership, gave me hope. Real love exists. Gentle love. Soulmate love. And because of you, I believe it's still possible.

To my cousin LaShandra "Shun"—thank you for being my bridge. The one who keeps me grounded and reminds me where I come from. Our bond is one of those rare gifts in life that doesn't need explanation. Just love. I thank you for always being a part of my heartbeat.

To my mentor and friend, Anne Elizabeth—you are light. Pure and intentional. You saw me through the different transitions of my life. You affirmed me when I was questioning myself. You never asked me to be anyone other than exactly who I am. Thank you for being a steady hand and a soft place to land.

To my sisterhood circle—Renee, Christina, and Latosha. Each of you, in your own way, has poured into me at moments when I didn't even realize how deeply I needed it. Your strength, your laughter, and your loyalty have meant everything. Thank you for holding space for me, for rooting for me, and for loving me through all my becoming.

To LaShunda Wilson, thank you for setting the tone of this book with such grace and intention. Your words held wisdom, depth, and compassion. You didn't just introduce my story, you honored it. I could not have asked for a more powerful way to welcome readers into these pages. Your voice brought light, and I'm so grateful you chose to share it.

To my beta readers—Rene, Yasmine, Terria, Christina, and Hope—thank you for bringing more than just your eyes to these pages. You showed up with your lived experience, professional insight, and deep care for the community. As early readers, you were not only beta readers but also powerful sensitivity and community readers. You held this work with integrity—reflecting back what landed, offering guidance where clarity was needed, and helping ensure that this book spoke with compassion to those it's meant to reach. Each of you brought something uniquely valuable: the perspective of women rooted in social work, education, justice systems, counseling, motherhood, healing, advocacy, and lived truth. You understood the heartbeat of these stories because you've lived through your own. And still, you read with empathy, challenged with care, and affirmed the purpose behind every chapter. Your feedback helped sharpen the message while protecting the emotional honesty of the journey. This book is stronger because of your voices—and I am forever grateful for how you walked with me in the becoming.

To the legendary authors Kimberla Lawson Roby and Beverly Jenkins—thank you for your generosity, your humility, and your willingness to share your wisdom with a new author just finding her way. When I reached out, you didn't hesitate. You answered with substance, encouragement, and sincerity—without the air of gatekeeping that often shadows this industry. Your kindness affirmed that sisterhood and legacy can coexist. I will forever be grateful for your light.

To my literary sisters, Yolanda and Lena—what a gift it is to journey through authorship alongside women who believe in purpose and power. Yolanda, thank you for your unwavering support, for patiently answering my questions, and for never making me feel like a burden. You extended sisterhood in the purest form—offering your platform to promote my book, making it your book of the month, and even allowing me the honor of being one of the first readers of two of your books. Our conversations, your encouragement, and your example have meant more to me than words can say. Lena, thank you for opening the door that helped me start telling my story publicly. Your collaboration came at just the right time. I am grateful for both of you—your light, your leadership, and your love.

To Tesuan and Iceberg Paris—thank you for using your platforms to highlight me and my author journey. You didn't just offer interviews—you offered space. Safe space. Celebratory space. Reflective space. You honored me, amplified my story, and made sure that others could witness this moment, too. I will never forget your kindness, your professionalism, and your generosity.

To my Heavenly Angels—Henry Allen, Rosie Leen Richardson, Andre Richardson, and Diane Mitchell. I feel you every day. In the unexpected moments of peace and in the strength I sometimes forget I carry. Your love left fingerprints on my soul, and I will carry you with me always. I pray I've made you proud.

And to every reader holding this book, you are part of my becoming. I wrote these pages for the little girl in me who dared to dream, but also for the woman in you who's learning to rise. May this journey remind you that your voice matters, your healing matters, and your story still holds power—even in the unfinished parts.

ABOUT THE AUTHOR

Victoria Sewell's journey is a testament to resilience and the power of storytelling. With over sixteen years of experience working across the education, social services, and justice fields, she is dedicated to fostering healing, empowerment, hope, and love.

Inspired by her early love for reading, journaling, and the arts, Victoria discovered a passion for writing that continues to shape her life's work. Her stories reflect a belief that even in life's hardest moments, there is room for redemption, grace, and growth.

In addition to her reflective and inspirational works, Victoria also writes fiction under the name Victoria Sewell Rose. Her debut novel, *Bella's Blues*, is an emotionally rich story of love, redemption, and second chances.

She is the founder of Mahogany Blue Publishing, where she uplifts authentic voices and stories that reflect resilience, hope, and love. Her books and publications honor the complexities of being human while encouraging readers to stand boldly in their truth.

When she's not writing, Victoria loves spending time with friends and family, experimenting with new recipes for Southern and Italian dishes, indulging her love of lemon cake and tiramisu, binge-watching favorite shows, enjoying old black and white films, and getting lost in a good romance novel.

Find out more at:

Website: victoriasewellrose.com

Facebook: AuthorVictoriaSewellRose

Instagram: victoriasewellrose_writes

TikTok: @victoriasewellrose

www.ingramcontent.com/pod-product-compliance
Lightning Source LLC
Chambersburg PA
CBHW021233130626
46554CB00004B/1474